# 75 Secondary Assembly Notes

## (Including 6th Form Assemblies)

## by Lawrie Baker

*(Former Head of Villiers High School, Southall)*

**W. Foulsham & Co. Ltd.**

London • New York • Toronto • Cape Town • Sydney

**W. FOULSHAM & CO. LIMITED**
Yeovil Road, Slough, Berks., England

# Acknowledgements

The author and publishers are grateful to the following for permission to reproduce material:
Oxford and Cambridge University Presses for extracts from The New English Bible second edition © 1970

The National Council of the Churches of Christ in the USA for Scripture quotations from the Revised Standard Version of the Bible © 1971 and 1952.

Jonathan Cape Ltd. for extracts from *The Complete Poems of W.H. Davies* and '*To Have or To Be*' by Erich Fromm.

Thorsons Publishing Group Ltd. for extracts from *Jonathan Livingston Seagull* by Richard Bach.

The Rev. Richard G. Jones for extracts from his verse '*God of Concrete, God of Steel*'.

The Estate of the late Sonia Brownell Orwell and Martin Secker & Warburg Ltd. for extracts from '*1984*' by George Orwell.

The Bodley Head for extracts from *Future Shock* by Alvin Toffler. Gill and Macmillan Ltd. for a prayer from 'Prayers of Life' by Michel Quoist.

ISBN 0–572–01513–5
Copyright © W. Foulsham & Co. Ltd. 1989

Printed and bound in Great Britain at The Bath Press, Avon

# Foreword

Taking an assembly is one task among the hundreds that many staff face each week. These teachers, often in a senior position, do not always have the time to spend in researching assembly material but, on the other hand, do not necessarily want to read something from a book.

These notes are intended to provide a framework, with a theme and a set of thoughts in logical sequence, within which those taking the assembly can express their own personality and ideas. That is why a space is provided at the end of each theme.

Grammatical convention has often been deliberately flouted in the usage of capital letters at the beginning of some words in order to give them prominence, and for ease of reference.

# CONTENTS

## 6th Form Assemblies

*Page*
*No.*

# RULES

**1** Have you been to a football/cricket/netball/hockey/tennis match lately? Or watched one on television?

**2** What would the match have been like if there had been no rules? Or if somebody had not insisted on the Rules being strictly kept?

**3** If Rules are broken something has to be done.

**4** So in life

Everything has Rules

**5** Some people call life a game.

Be careful – it is serious.

It is THE game.

**6** In life people

a) Make Rules

b) Change Rules

c) Break Rules

**7** Some say get rid of the Rules

but you cannot.

**8** If you get rid of the present Rules, others have to take their place.

**9** There is a famous set of Rules in the Bible called the Ten Commandments.

**10** Exodus 21

(i) No other Gods beside the one true God
(ii) No graven image
(iii) Not to take God's name in vain
(iv) Keep the Sabbath Day holy – no work
(v) Honour your Father and Mother
(vi) Do not kill
(vii) Do not commit adultery
(viii) Do not steal
(ix) Do not commit perjury (do not lie)
(x) Do not covet (want what others have).

**11** Four are religious, but six are practical Rules for living.

**12** Probably last is least kept. Cause of most of our problems today:

Wanting what others have

6

**13** Television is the great tempter: Advertisements

> Lovely Houses
> Lovely Holidays
> Lovely Cars
> Lots of Money

**14** People want a lot more and do not care how they get it.

**15** So stealing has got worse and worse.

**16** (Give examples – if any in School – or from Newspapers/TV etc).

**17** Few seem to think stealing is wrong, they call it *lifting, nicking, acquiring*.

**18** It is wrong anywhere and at any time, but particularly evil within the very community in which we live and work.

**19** This school is a community and it can only work if we can all trust one another.

**20** Unfortunately there are a number of people who only believe in the eleventh Commandment:

> You must not be caught.

**21** Stealing is evil – if you steal STOP IT NOW.

**PRAYER**

The people of old based their lives on the Ten Commandments. Let us tread the path of purity and trustworthiness and shun the way of dishonesty and covetousness.

---

NOTES – RULES

---

# BEGINNING OF NEW TERM

1  First question, are you glad to be back?

2  Some will say 'yes', many may say 'no'.
   (I wonder what the teachers would say?)

3  Those pupils who answer yes, say

   a) I like it here
   b) I get bored during holidays
   c) My friends are here
   d) I don't mind school work
   e) I like holidays, but enough is enough.

4  The last one is the problem really – enough is enough. However pleasurable an activity, it can become boring after time.

   a) Those who work say, 'I wish I could stop work.'
   b) Those who can't get a job feel worthless and purposeless and say, 'If only I could get a job.'

5  Most people agree : there is so much to do and so little time to do it in.

6  A lot of our life is spent doing useless things.

7  There is a Greek legend called:

   'THE MYTH OF SISYPHUS'
   Before dying Sisyphus asked his wife not to pay him Funeral Honours, but once in the Underworld he went to Hades to complain of his wife's negligence. He asked permission to go back to Earth for a moment to punish her. Permission was granted. Back on Earth, Sisyphus refused to return to the Underworld. Sisyphus was punished for bad faith by being condemned eternally to roll up the slope of a mountain an enormous boulder. Each time it nearly reached the summit it rolled down again.

8  Sometimes life seems like that. Not getting anywhere. Constant repetition of same tasks – 'The Daily Round' eg morning to work : evening home. 5 days' work, 2 days' holiday. And for what?

9  So to return to the original question: Am I glad to be back?

   a) In one sense 'No' – love holidays, freedom, travel, relaxation.
   b) In another 'Yes' – job satisfaction, purpose, status [explain], friends.

10  And so there's not one answer

We need work, and
We need relaxation

11   How much of each is the real question.

**PRAYER**

O God, may we be glad that we have work to do. Help us to carry it out to the best of our ability so that when it's finished, we may enjoy our rest and relaxation.

---

NOTES – BEGINNING OF NEW TERM

---

# FASTING

1   Almost every magazine has articles on 'Diet'.

How to keep healthy
Cut down on carbohydrates
             cholesterol
             alcohol
Be regular in our exercise – jog, swim, run etc.

2   This all takes willpower.

        Can I be strong enough?
        Am I too lazy?
        Can I be bothered?

3   Most religions include idea of disciplining body and mind.

4   In fact many religious rules demand:

        strength of mind; willpower

5   Some religions suggest simple diets.

        No alcohol, no pork, no beef, etc.

6   Muslim Holy Book – Quran – says:

        "Eat and drink but be not wasteful."

**7**  But today we are going to concentrate on religious idea of Fasting.

**8**  What is its purpose?

It is to make people realise their many blessings and is a means of showing thanksgiving and gratitude to God.

**9**  *For Muslim*: Ramadhan is the month of Fasting (the date varies each year). Ramadhan is one of Islam's Five Pillars of Wisdom.

Fasting is prescribed:
> 'So that you may guard against Evil.'

**10**  *For Hindu*: Navaratri (nine nights), part of Festival of Dussehra. In Punjab includes seven nights of fasting.

**11**  *For Jew*: Yom Kippur – the Day of Atonement – observed as Fast until nightfall.

During these 25 hours most Jewish people remain in Synagogue. No food or drink touches their lips.

This is to show they are sorry for all evil done during year.

**12**  *For Christian*: Period of Lent in February.

Ash Wednesday is day of Fasting for strict Christians. Saying sorry for one's sins.

**13**  Whether religious or not, we should realise most of us **overeat**:
> two thirds of world is hungry

**14**  Disciplining oneself is good in itself. So easy to be indulgent, to let oneself go.

Every now and again we need to prove to ourselves we can control ourselves.

**PRAYER**

Help us to control our thoughts, our actions, our appetites. Teach us the value of good habits with healthy minds and bodies.

NOTES – FASTING

# NOVEMBER

**1** Famous poem of Thomas Hood called 'NO'

> No Sun, No Moon,
> No Morn, No Noon,
> No Dawn, No Dusk,
> No proper time of Day,
> No warmth, No cheerfulness, No healthful ease,
> No comfortable feel in any member,
> No shade, No shine, No Butterflies, No Bees,
> No Fruit, No Flowers, No Leaves, No Birds,
> November!

**2** November seems a dark, miserable month but it is famous for three very important events in Medical History:

**A**    On the 7th November 1867 Marie Curie was born. Her name then was:

Marya Sklodovska

Born in Warsaw, capital of Poland.

Fascinated by her Father's glass case filled with scientific instruments.

But learning difficult. Russians ruled over Poland and Polish children not encouraged to learn.

But Marya was determined.

Aged 24 she went to Paris to study. There Marya became Marie. Met Pierre Curie, a French scientist, and married him.

Both became interested in a substance which gave off rays. They wanted to know how to get 'Pure Radium' – as they called it.

After several years of hard work they were successful.

Radium became very valuable in curing certain diseases.

In 1906 Pierre was run over by a wagon and died.

Marie continued until 1934 when she died from the effects of exposure to radio-activity.

**B**    On the 8th November 1895, Professor Wilhelm Röntgen had been reading a book and laid it down with a key in it as a bookmark.

Absentmindedly he put an electric tube (known as a Crookes Tube) on the book, which was by chance resting on a photographic plate.

When he moved the tube and the book, he found he had a picture of the key on the photographic plate.

He tried it again – same result.

If rays can pass through a book – why not metals?

If through metals – why not bodies?

Röntgen proved his rays could pass through flesh and photograph bones, etc.

Did not know what to call rays:

$X = $ '*Unknown*' – called them X-Rays.

C    Professor James Simpson of Glasgow asked two friends to an unusual party.

Each had a bottle in front of them.

Sat, talked, breathed fumes from bottle, conversation became livelier, all talked at once and then all three became unconscious.

On waking all were delighted – because this was a test.

Bottles contained chloroform. Simpson believed this could be used for Operations.

Until then (except for *ether* in USA) limbs were sawn off, to the accompaniment of dreadful screams.

On 12th November 1847, chloroform was first used as an Anaesthetic in an operation in Britain.

## PRAYER

Let us remember in our prayers all those we know who are ill or injured and ask God to restore them to full health.
We are thankful for all the wonderful discoveries of medical science, which have resulted in better care of the sick, greater relief from pain, new cures and the prolonging of life.

---

NOTES – NOVEMBER

---

# CHRISTMAS ORIGINS

1    Christmas is a mixture of many different celebrations and traditions.

a) Yule – Mid-winter pagan festival – 3 days.

Central feature: burning of Yule Log.

Time of feasting, drinking, singing.
People retold the legends about Thor and Odin – the Gods to whom Yule was dedicated.
Sprigs of Mistletoe – a sacred plant – were ceremoniously cut.

b) Saturnalia – Roman Mid-winter festival – 7 days.

In honour of Saturn.
Time of unrestrained merry-making.
Early Christians found this pagan festival, already a holiday, a good opportunity to celebrate Christ's birth.
Presents and greetings were given.

c) Sinter Klaas – ancient Bishop St. Nicholas, of Asia Minor. Presents were put in a shoe.

**2**  But above all Christmas is a Christian festival.

Christ Mass – the Festival of Christ. For Christians it is the coming of God into human flesh.

Not as a full-grown man in royal robes – but as a baby.

Christ – Christos – The Messiah – God's chosen one – The Anointed.

**3**  In many Churches there will be a crib with the baby in a manger watched over by Mary and Joseph, accompanied by angels and animals.

**4**  There was no room in the inn.

**5**  At Christmas we remember:

a) Children – particularly those who are unwanted or badly treated.
b) All those who are lonely, suffering hardship or discomfort.

**6**  At Christmas we give generously to help those less fortunate than ourselves.

**PRAYER**

We give thanks for the coming of Jesus Christ into the world. We pray that the joy His Coming brings to Christmas may be shared by all, so that Christmas may be a time of happiness and goodwill.

NOTES – CHRISTMAS ORIGINS

# CHRISTMAS GIVING

READING: St Luke, Chapter 2, verses 1–20

1   Christmas is celebration of birth of Jesus.

> Christ = Messiah = Anointed
>
> Mass = Celebration.

2   Anointed. The Old Testament Kings were anointed with oil poured over their heads.

3   Christmas then is the story of a King.

4   But it is the story of a *Baby* born as a King.

> A special baby.

5   Christians believe God came into this world as a human being and yet remained as God.

> A mystery (all religions have them).

6   Jesus best described as God – Man.

This means Jesus remained fully God but also became fully Man.

He cannot be less of each. God and Man are interwoven in Him.

7   So when people say 'I'll only believe in God when I see him,'

the Christian says 'We have seen him – in Jesus.'

8   The story of Christmas is a lovely one.

> All religions enjoy it.
> A baby,
> A young Mum and Dad.
> The animals in the cattle shed.
> The Angels singing.
> The Star shining.
> The Shepherds watching.
> The Wise Men bringing gifts.

9   Christmas is a time of happiness, light, joy, peace, goodwill.

10   What are you going to do to spread a little happiness this Christmas?

11   There are children in need:

> Dr Barnardo's.
> National Children's Homes
> Save The Children Fund.

12  There are numerous charity Christmas cards.

13  There are old people's homes to visit.

14  Let us remember Christmas is the time of giving:

God gave himself to the world.

Let us give something in return.

**PRAYER**

We rejoice at the coming of God into this world in the human form of Jesus Christ. May we understand the meaning of Christmas and with understanding may we give ourselves to the service of others.

NOTES – CHRISTMAS GIVING

# CHRISTMAS STARS

READING: St Matthew, Chapter 2, verses 1–12 (New English Bible)

1  Stars have always fascinated people.

Study of stars for themselves = Astronomy
Study of stars for their influence = Astrology.

2  Magazines and popular newspapers almost always have:

'Your Stars/Horoscope.'

3  It is the first thing many people read.

4  In the Christmas Story three Wise Men saw a rising star.

For **Wise Men** – read **Astrologers**.

5  Astronomers now believe there was an extraordinary star at the time Jesus was born – possibly a fusion of two stars.

6  This phenomenon has been repeated since, at intervals of hundreds of years.

7  The Astrologers followed the star and came to Bethlehem.

**8**   They gave the Baby three gifts.

They were symbolic.

**9**   Gold – because he was King.

Frankincense – because he was God.

Myrrh (used to anoint bodies) – because Jesus was going to die.

**10**   When they saw the star they were overjoyed, because it was a star of hope.

**11**   Hope is the message of Christmas.

**12**   The world is full of:

> Poverty
> Disease
> Famine
> Earthquakes
> Cruelty
> Brutality
> Injustice
> Violence
> War
> Murder

**13**   People need hope and Christmas brings that message.

**14**   The Angels sang:

> 'Peace on Earth
> Goodwill to all people.'

**15**   What a wonderful message for the world.

**16**   What a pity it does not last the whole year.

**PRAYER**

The Star of Bethlehem brought hope and joy to the world. May we, O God, through the light of that Star, give hope and joy to others this Christmastime.

---

NOTES – CHRISTMAS STARS

---

# NEW YEAR RESOLUTIONS

1   Another new year.

2   Resolutions are made at New Year:

eg Never to be late, not to bite one's nails.

3   Often hopeless – they last hours/days/weeks.

4   This year I am going to suggest a Resolution for you.

5   First a story from the Bible:

*DAVID v GOLIATH (I SAMUEL 17)*
*DAVID*      –   Young Hebrew Shepherd Boy
*GOLIATH*  –   Huge Philistine Giant
              Height 6 cubits 1 span

6 cubits = 8 ft (2.40 m)
1 span = 9 ins (22.5 cm)

Total = 8 ft 9 ins (2.625 m)

6   Story: Two armies lined up.

Every hour Giant came out and challenged Hebrews.
David went to King : 'Let me fight him.'
King Saul said     : 'You have not got a chance. He has got height,
                      helmet, armour, shield, huge sword.'
David said         : 'Do not worry, I have a plan.'

7   The Giant challenged again.

8   David chose 5 smooth stones from a stream and put them in his bag.

9   He went forward, took out a stone, put it in his sling and slung it. It hit the Giant on his temple, sank in and killed him.

10   Was this luck? No.

It was brain over brawn. David had noticed a gap between the Giant's helmet and his nose guard.

11   What has this story got to do with New Year Resolutions?

12   Everything.

This year I want you to resolve to have confidence in yourself.

13  You can win in the battle of life – even, like David, against hopeless odds.

14  It is amazing what you can do if you believe in yourself.

15  So your New Year Resolution must be:

'I can and I will succeed'

**PRAYER**

We ask that we may have confidence in ourselves and may present ourselves at our best to others. We need patience and perseverance in order to achieve our goals in the days ahead.

---

NOTES – NEW YEAR RESOLUTIONS

---

# NEW YEAR RETROSPECTIVE

1  What advantage to have eyes in the back of your head.
   Marvellous for teachers.

2  Romans had a god called Janus.
   God of Doorways, gates and all beginnings.

3  Often shown with two faces, one at front of head, one at back.

4  Romans called him the 'Doorkeeper'.
   He would open door to let old year out and new year in.

5  From Janus we get *Janitor* – Doorkeeper.
   But we also get January.

**6**  Strange thing is the Roman Calendar began in March, not January.

**7**  For us January is beginning of year and, if you like, Janus opens door.

**8**  Looking back, what about last year?

What was it like for you?
So good it can never be bettered?
So terrible it is a good job it is gone?
Nothing special either way?

**9**  Whatever, it will never return.

'Time and Tide wait for no one.'
What happened is over and done with.

**10**  This is a sad lesson of life. So often we look back and wish we could have a replay.

As they are able to in programmes like 'It'll be Alright on the Night.'

**11**  If only we could have a few rehearsals until we get it right.

**12**  With hindsight we can say:

'I shouldn't have done that'
'I shouldn't have said that'

*or*

'I wish I had said that or done that.'

**13**  But it is gone and finished with, so let's use Janus' other face and look forward to this year.

**14**  It's a blank page on which to write our story.

But the page can quickly be blotted or stained.

**15**  So what will this year have in store for us?

A great deal will depend on *you*.
Things do not just happen – most often they are the result of some action of ours.

**16**  Of course, there are things out of our control – strokes of luck, sometimes good, sometimes bad.

**17**  A belief in God is a help.

To believe we are not on our own, struggling against hopeless odds.

**18**  The door to the year is an entrance, as King George V (the present Queen's grand- father) said when he read these words, by H.L. Haskins, in his Christmas Broadcast:

"And I said to the man who stood at the Gate of Year: Give me a light that I may tread safely into the unknown!" and he replied:

"Go out into the darkness and put thine hand into the hand of God. That shall be to thee better than light and safer than a known way."

NOTES – NEW YEAR RETROSPECTIVE

# CHINESE NEW YEAR

1   The Festival of The Chinese New Year can last up to a fortnight.

It takes place between mid-January and mid-February.

2   Fascinating going up to Chinatown in London (or the Chinese districts of other cities) and visiting the restaurants and supermarkets.

3   The Chinese seem a very gentle race.

Who in England complains about them? When have they caused any trouble?

(Perhaps we should remember this, when complaining of immigrants).

4   Like many other people, the Chinese celebrate New Year with new clothes, clean houses and lanterns.

5   One special feature is the Lion Dance.

Firecrackers (they were once called 'Chinese Crackers') are let off to frighten away the evil spirits.

6   Perhaps most important thing about Chinese Year is each is dedicated to one of 12 animals.

Rat, Ox, Tiger, Rabbit (Hare), Dragon, Snake, Horse, Sheep, Monkey, Cockerel, Dog, Pig.

7   Why in that order?

Old legend. 12 animals arguing about name of next year. Each thought it should have *its* name.

So decided on race across river.

Ox in lead, but did not notice Rat on back. At the bank Rat jumped off and landed first. Others finished in order given above.

8   Chinese people believe you inherit characteristics of animal of year of birth:

| 1970 | 1982 | The Dog | 1976 | 1988 | The Dragon |
|------|------|---------|------|------|------------|
| 1971 | 1983 | The Pig | 1977 | 1989 | The Snake |
| 1972 | 1984 | The Rat | 1978 | 1990 | The Horse |
| 1973 | 1985 | The Ox | 1979 | 1991 | The Sheep |
| 1974 | 1986 | The Tiger | 1980 | 1992 | The Monkey |
| 1975 | 1987 | The Rabbit (The Hare) | 1981 | 1993 | The Cockerel |

9   So this new Chinese Year is the Year of :

(name according to list).

10   What was the animal of your Year of Birth?

Were you A Dog? A Horse? A Snake? A Dragon?

11   What are the characteristics of a Dog?

Faithfulness, affection, protector.

12   What about a Pig?

A much maligned animal. It is actually very clean. Is its characteristic *persistence*?

13   Whole idea of characteristics at birth is interesting. Many believe in birth signs.

14   This area of interest is called Astrology.

Astrologers read the stars.
Astronomers study them.

15   No popular paper or magazine would be without its 'Horoscope.'

People believe in their star signs.

16   So perhaps the Chinese are right, it does matter when you are born.

Some people believe it even matters whether you were born during the night or during the day.

17   The wonderful thing is we are all different.

No one else in the world quite like us.

**18** That is why many people would say:

It is not chance, not the stars, not the animal of a particular year but God who gives us each a unique individuality, a Human Soul.

**PRAYER**

We are thankful for the lessons we learn from other people in the world.

Above all, we marvel at human life and the miracle of our uniqueness as individuals.

NOTES – CHINESE NEW YEAR

# NEWSPAPERS

**1** Do you read a Newspaper?

Do you believe it?

**2** I have brought a selection of this morning's/yesterday's newspapers.

What is the main story of each?
What are the other main stories?

**3** Is this *THE* news?

or is it *THEIR* news?

**4** The facts are presented selectively.

(*Try to find a story that is treated quite differently in different newspapers*).

**5** What kind of news?

Why is the news nearly always about bad things: crashes, disasters, crime, violence?

(Do the stories today/yesterday bear this out?)

**6** There are a million stories out there – so why these?

**7** Because these stories sell papers.

**8** This says a great deal about the public – about us.

**9** All the good things:

> charity, helping old people, deeds of bravery, the worthwhile activities of young people –

these are often neglected.

**10** It is so easy to believe that newspapers tell us the truth.

**11** We must remember that papers tell us what they want us to believe.

**12** We are often tempted to say: 'Of course it is true, I read it in the newspaper.'

**13** The inaccuracies are revealed when the story is about something or someone we know –

> The name can be wrong, the address, the numbers involved,
>
> *but more importantly*
>
> only half the facts, and even those mis-reported.

**14** Let us be very careful when reading newspapers.

Look at them critically.
Make our own judgements.

**PRAYER**

We give thanks for the printed word and particularly for newspapers which can provide valuable information as well as give pleasure.

May newspaper editors act responsibly and we, as readers, be more critical of what we read.

---

NOTES – NEWSPAPERS

---

# GOING ON TO EMPLOYMENT

1   How many are thinking about employment (the work or job they will do)?

2   For some, of course, tragically, it may be unemployment.

3   If you are going to Further/Higher Education, employment may seem a long way off.

4   Are you thinking either now or eventually of going into industry or commerce?

        Probably not.

5   For many the height of success is to get into one of the professions: –

        Medicine
        Dentistry
        Law
        Accountancy
        Teaching

6   Why is this?

    a) Do the professions have better working conditions?
       (Hospital doctors do 80 hours per week).
    b) Is the pay better?
       Not for many (nurses, hospital doctors).

7   What is it then?

        Is it the status?
        The opinion/regard of society?

Even agriculture has a better image than industry/commerce.

8   Industrial Revolution, late 18th Century-early 19th Century.

Not welcomed by everybody.

9   The slight of : "He's in Trade."

10  Industry has been given a bad name – unfairly.

11  Schools have been very resistant to preparing pupils for work in industry.

At last we have accepted the word 'Training'.

In these last few years:

        TVEI, CPVE

We have become Technical, Pre-vocational and Vocational.

12　Education and Industry need to be brought closer and closer together.

13　Industry and Commerce offer exciting possibilities of which most of us are ignorant:

eg Cleaning Science, Food Technology.

14　Typical story is of woman who said of her two daughters:

'Jean has done well, she's gone into Nursing, but I'm afraid Julie has only gone into M & S.'

15　Universities and Polytechnics are now seeking the advantages of links with industry and offering *Applied* Degrees.

16　In the end it is industry that creates the wealth of the country.

**PRAYER**

O God, bless the fruits of honest labour and help industry to prosper through wise decisions and just dealing. We remember with compassion those that are unemployed and pray that those who have the responsibility for the economy of the nation may find solutions to the curse of unemployment.

---

NOTES – GOING ON TO EMPLOYMENT

---

# VIOLENCE

1　We live in a violent society:

　　Streets
　　Playgrounds
　　Football Stadiums
　　War, Shootings.

2　Not only so, but we see it on television, all in close up – often repeated over and over again:–

The pool of blood
The bullet holes
The old person's stitches
The grief of relatives.

3  Why are people so violent?

Frustration
Boredom
'Gives you a Kick'

4  Human beings can be pretty horrible, some people actually enjoy it.

eg recent attacks on children and old people.

5  A great deal is mindless – no sense in it.

6  But some is done because it seems to pay.

7  In some senses – yes it does:

War
Robbery – Mugging
Terrorism.

8  But limited and short-term.

A selfish gain for individual or group.

9  Violence has seeds of its own destruction in it.

Civilisation, as we know it, could be in jeopardy.

10  Is non-violence stupidity?

11  Are followers of Peace Movements in a lost cause?

12  Let us listen to Mahatma Gandhi:

'Literally speaking non-violence means non-killing. But it really means that you may not offend anybody. This is an ideal which we have to reach and it is an ideal to be reached even at this very moment, if we are capable of doing so. But it is not a proposition in geometry, it is not even like solving difficult problems in higher mathematics – it is infinitely more difficult . . . You will have to pass many a sleepless night and go through many a mental torture before you can even be within measurable distance of this goal.'

13  This could mean your own injury, harm, death.

14  Is this an impossible ideal?

15  Gandhi would say such sacrifice is the only way to save the world.

**PRAYER**

Give us the courage to practise non-violence and to resist retaliation.

May we bear in mind the words of Gandhi:

'NON-VIOLENCE IS THE WEAPON OF THE STRONGEST AND BRAVEST.'

---

NOTES – VIOLENCE

---

# HUNGER

1   Did you have a good Breakfast?

2   Do you get hungry – really hungry?

Most of us do not know what real hunger is.

3   We need 2,500 calories a day.

(Calorie: unit of heat for energy and warmth).

4   Average daily intake of calories:

| | |
|---|---|
| U.S.A. | 3,300 Calories |
| U.K. | 3,190 Calories |
| Portugal | 2,770 Calories |
| Zambia | 2,590 Calories |
| Zaire | 2,060 Calories |
| Bangladesh | 1,840 Calories |

5   At least 500 million people go to bed hungry every night.

(1 in 8 of the world's population).

**6** Dead:   1st World War           :  8 million
             Bangladesh Cyclone  : 1/4 million
             Starvation **every month**  : 1/4 million

**7** Some of us have far too much.

       Butter mountain
       Grain mountain
       Milk lake etc.

**8** Often cheaper to throw away than send to a starving country,

eg Shiploads of Potatoes tipped into the ocean, Crops ploughed in.

**9** 'Poor' for the Third World means:

       No Food
       No Shelter
       No Drink
       Death

**10** So what can be done?

  i) Government Aid – not only food but machinery, technology, education.
  ii) Voluntary help – e.g. Band Aid, Live Aid, Save The Children Fund, Oxfam etc.

**11** But we are only scratching the surface.

Problems: Distribution – terrain, bandits
          Political strife
          Geography – rain, desert etc.
          Disasters.

**12** Greatest problem now is Africa.

**13** Policy of encouraging poorer countries to grow exportable cash crops to earn foreign exchange to pay for imports.

**14** *But* soaring prices mean many developing countries cannot afford to foot the bill of imports.

**15** Policy now being questioned:

Local and small-scale food production seen as crucial in eradicating hunger and raising incomes of rural poor.

**PRAYER**

We give thanks for our daily food and the advantages of living in a climate that provides plentiful crops. We remember those in other parts of the world who have little to eat or even worse, are starving. Bless all those who through money, research, education or the commitment of their own lives and talents are helping to reduce starvation and poverty in the world.

NOTES – HUNGER

# MONEY

1   The world is obsessed with money.

2   Understandably, as everybody needs it.

3   Once upon a time you could barter,

    e.g. A sack of flour for a horse.

4   Stop and think how many things you could get now without money – not many.

5   Then think of how many more things you could get if you had lots of money.

6   Look at this £5 note.

      Where has it been?
      What has it done?
      What could I do if I had a sack of them?

7   In 1954 a French Priest from Le Havre wrote a book of prayers called '*Prayers Of Life*.'

8   His name was Michel Quoist.

9   One prayer he wrote was called:

      'A Prayer Before A £5 Note'

10  Listen to it:

      'Lord, see this note, it frightens me.
      You know its secrets, you know its history.

How heavy it is!
It scares me, for it cannot speak
It will never tell all it hides in its creases.

It is heavy, heavy Lord.
It fills me with awe, it frightens me
For it has death on its conscience,
All the poor fellows who killed themselves for it,
To possess it for a few hours,
To have through it a little pleasure, a little joy,
a little life . . .

Through how many hands has it passed, Lord?
And what has it done in the course of its long silent
trips?
It has offered white roses to the radiant fiancée.
It has paid for the Baptismal Party, and fed the
growing baby.
It has provided bread for the family table.
Because of it there was laughter among the young, and
joy among the adults.
It has paid for the saving visit of the doctor.
It has bought the book that taught the youngster.
It has clothed the young girl.

But it has sent the letter breaking the engagement.
It has paid for the death of a child in its mother's
womb.
It has bought the liquor that made the drunkard.
It has produced the film unfit for children,
And has recorded the indecent song.
It has broken the morals of the adolescent and made of
the adult a thief.
It has bought for a few hours the body of a woman.
It has paid for the weapons of the crime and for the
wood of a coffin.'

11    Money can be used for wonderful things. But it can also be used for terrible
things.

12    The Bible says: "The *Love* of money is the root of all evil" – not money itself.

13    We need to learn to put it to good use.

**PRAYER** (Michel Quoist)

O Lord, I offer you this note with its joyous mysteries, its sorrowful mysteries.

I thank you for all the life and joy it has given.

I ask your forgiveness for the harm it has done.

But above all, Lord, I offer it to you as a symbol of all the labours of men,
indestructible money, which tomorrow will be changed into eternal life.

# GOOD AND EVIL

**1** There are two sides to human nature

The good and the evil.

**2** There are different views:

a) We are born perfect but society corrupts us.
b) There is an inbuilt tendency to evil which is born in us.

**3** Religious people have always been conscious of evil.

**4** Christians call it sin,

i.e. Doing what God does not want us to do.
Doing what God disapproves of.

**5** Many religions have strict rules:

e.g.  Islam
Judaism
Christianity.

**6** They say what one must do:

a) To please God
b) To be happy
c) To live after death or to return to this life (reincarnation)

**7** Some religions believe that there are evil spirits which lead us astray:

Satan, The Devil, Siva.

31

8   Even people who are not religious, such as Humanists, believe humans must struggle to overcome evil and strive towards perfection.

9   In each of us there is a constant battle being waged between Good and Evil.

10   There is a passage in the Bible which puts it this way:

'The Good which I want to do I fail to do. But what I do is the wrong which is against my will. When I want to do the right only the wrong is within my reach.

Right down inside me I delight in the Law of God, but I find that in my body there is a different view.'

(ROMANS 7).

11   Religious people believe they cannot win the fight without God, helped by Jesus or Mohammed, the Gurus or Buddha.

12   Some people never fight the battle at all.

13   Unfortunately if you do not fight, evil always wins.

14   What about you?

> Are you fighting?
> Are you better than last year?
> Do you put your mistakes right?

15   Or, are you happy just being bad, unpleasant, unkind and hateful?

**PRAYER**

We ask for strength to fight evil and uphold what is good. Let us not harm others by our words or deeds but be kind, thoughtful, honest and true.

---

NOTES – GOOD AND EVIL

---

# HISTORY OF JUDAISM

1   Judaism is one of the major religions of the world.

2   Earlier the Jews were called Hebrews, possibly originally from a tribe called Habiru.

3   Hebrew is the language of the Old Testament – the Jews' Holy Book – and of Orthodox Jews.

4   The story of the Hebrews really begins with Abraham who lived in a place called Ur of the Chaldees, on the fringes of desert country, in which the inhabitants roamed to find pasture for animals.

5   We are told he left the country because he wanted to get away from worship of the Moon, to seek one true God.

6   The name of God is too holy to be written or spoken by Jews.

7   As there were no vowels in the Bible Hebrew text and J and Y, and V and W are confused, nobody really knows how the Hebrew God's name was written. Without vowels it is either:

   JHVH or YHWH

8   Putting the vowels in it, it becomes:

   JEHOVAH or YAHWEH

9   The story of Abraham and his descendants, the Israelites, is told in the first five Books of the Old Testament which are called the Torah (The Law).

10   The second Book, Exodus, Chapter 21, contains the famous Ten Commandments.

11   The fifth Book – Deuteronomy – sums up many laws and attitudes.

Listen to a passage (Deuteronomy 10, verses 12–13).

'And now, Israel, what doth the Lord require of thee, but to fear the Lord thy God, to walk in all his ways, and to love him and to serve the Lord thy God with all thy heart and with all thy soul, to keep the Commandments of the Lord and his statutes, which I command thee this day for thy good?'

12   The Jewish calendar is counted from when the Jews believed the world was created.

The New Year falls in the Autumn.

In 1987 it was the Jewish Year 5748.

13   The Jewish calendar is based on the Moon.

12 Lunar months = 354 days, so an extra month is added seven times in every 19 years.

**14** The tenth day of the New Year is Yom Kippur - Day of Atonement.

**15** Atonement = at-one-ment. Being reconciled to God and ridding oneself of sin.

**16** The sins of the people in the Old Testament were confessed by the priest over a goat which was released into the wilderness.

The Escape-Goat or 'Scapegoat.'

**17** On Yom Kippur the Jews eat and drink nothing but spend the day in prayer, confessing their sins.

**PRAYER**

(From Psalm 51).

Be merciful to me, O God, because of your constant love, because of your great mercy wipe away my sins! . . . I have sinned against you – only against you – and done what you consider evil. . . . . . Create a pure heart in me, O God, and put a new and loyal spirit in me.

---

NOTES – HISTORY OF JUDAISM

---

# JUDAISM – CHANUKKAH

**1** Jewish Festival of Light is called:

CHANUKKAH

**2** Lasts eight days and nights. Usually in December. Celebrates triumph of Good over Evil 2,000 years ago.

**3** Antiochus of Syria then ruled Holy Land. He forbade Jews to worship Yahweh.

Destroyed Sacred Scrolls and desecrated Temple by putting statues of Zeus in it.

**4** A resistance group led by Judas Maccabeus – ('The Hammer') fought Emperor.

**5** Long, bitter struggle but eventually Syrians were defeated and Judas led his followers into Jerusalem.

**6** Judas cleansed the Temple, but there was only enough pure oil to keep Temple light burning for one night. By a miracle the light burnt for eight nights.

That is why Chanukkah lasts eight days.

**7** In Synagogue, as well as in home, a special eight-branched candlestick is used. (There is actually a ninth holder from which others are lit).

**8** On first night one candle is lit, on second another and so on until all eight are alight.

**9** In daily services as each candle is lit special prayers are recited and Psalms 113–118 are read.

**10** Chanukkah (= Dedication) is a happy festival.

Presents are exchanged, games played.

**11** One traditional game is played with a four-sided spinning-top called adreidel. Each side has a Hebrew letter – N, G, H and SH. These stand for: 'Nes Gadol Hayah Sham' (A great miracle happened there).

**12** The traditional food is Latkes, potato cakes made with cheese.

**13** Focus of Festival is the Menorah (eight branched candlestick) which is displayed prominently reminding them of the Miracle of the Light and the victory of Light over Darkness.

PRAYER

(From Psalms 113 and 115).

Not unto us, O Lord, but unto thy name give glory for thy mercy, and for thy truth's sake.

From the rising of the sun unto the going down of the same the Lord's name is to be praised.

NOTES – JUDAISM-CHANUKKAN

# NOBEL PRIZES

1   Each year the world has a Prize Day.

Prizes worth thousands of pounds.

2   These prizes are the Nobel Prizes given to those who have done most to benefit mankind in Science, Literature and Peace.

3   Alfred Nobel was born in Sweden on 21st October, 1833 and died on 10th December, 1896.

4   Nobel's father was an inventor and was interested in explosives.

Alfred shared his father's interest and experimented with Nitro-Glycerine.

He found he could explode this under water.

5   But Nitro-Glycerine was dangerously unreliable and liable to explode accidently.

6   By chance Alfred Nobel managed to discover a way of making Nitro-Glycerine in a solid form. This was called Dynamite and Alfred Nobel was its inventor.

7   Alfred made a lot of money out of Dynamite. But his conscience told him that war was wrong and he decided to try to help bring about a lasting peace.

8   Thus he arranged for three world prizes to be awarded annually.

9   The one that has the greatest respect is the prize for Peace.

10   A good example is the prize announced on 10th October, 1976. It was to two women from Northern Ireland, Betty Williams and Mairead Corrigan.

11   One day in August 1976 a get-away car carrying terrorists smashed into and killed 3 children, aged 8 years, 2 years and 6 weeks.

12   Like the Remembrance Day killing at Enniskillen, everybody was shocked.

13   Mairead Corrigan, the Aunt of the 3 dead children and Betty Williams, a Mother of 3, decided to form the Ulster Peace Movement.

14   On receiving the award, Mairead said:

'Nobel was the man who invented Dynamite. We hope to change things without Dynamite.'

15   Violence in Ireland continues, so what has been achieved?

16   Things do not happen overnight.

It is a contribution, that is all.

**17** But it is a *women's* contribution.

So often women have brought sense to a situation.

**PRAYER**

TIME OF QUIET

Let us in the quietness think about:

Northern Ireland ⎫ (*substitute the problems at the time of the Assembly.*)
Lebanon ⎬
Afghanistan ⎭

Finally, let us not only *think* about these problems but determine to contribute in some small way to their solution.

---

NOTES – NOBEL PRIZES

---

# CHRISTIAN PERIOD OF LENT

**1** The first day of Lent is Ash Wednesday.

**2** The day before is called Shrove Tuesday.

**3** 'Shriven' is to be absolved from one's sins.

Shrove Tuesday is a day of preparation for Lent.

**4** On Shrove Tuesday, all fats in the house are used up. The Pancake is a symbol of this.

**5** Ash Wednesday begins the Fasting of Lent.

There are 40 days from Ash Wednesday to Good Friday or 'Holy' Friday.

**6** Lent is a time for self-denial.

Resisting of temptation.

**7** People give up things for Lent:

eg sweets, smoking etc.

**8** How did this all begin?

**9** Listen to the story from the Bible:

(St Matthew, Chapter 4, verses 1–11).

**10** Jesus was 30 years old and just beginning to preach.

**11** (a) He went away on his own.
(b) He fasted.
(c) He thought about his life and work.
(d) He was tempted.

**12** Jesus was really asking himself the question:

'What sort of Messiah (or Christ) am I going to be?'

**13** (a) 'Turn the stones into bread.'

To give people material things.

Jesus was very hungry.

Thousands of others were very hungry. Give them bread – is that the answer?

(b) 'Jump off the top of the Temple.'

Amaze people with miracles – is that the answer?

(c) 'Rule all the Kingdoms of the world.'

Be a military leader, conquer the world – is that the answer?

**14** But Jesus rejected all these.

(a) Material – bread is not enough. The people need spiritual food.

(b) Magical – people would come to see his miracles but not be led to God.

(c) Military – you cannot conquer the world without worshipping Satan – in other words 'doing Evil.'

**15** Jesus decided he was going to:

Preach love.
Tell people about his Father, God.
Sacrifice himself.

**16** And that is why he allowed himself to be crucified on Good Friday.

**17**  By it he has shown the Love of God to the world.

**18**  The Cross is the symbol of Christianity.

**PRAYER**

We pray for the courage to resist temptation and the power to renew ourselves in God's service.

---

NOTES – CHRISTIAN PERIOD OF LENT

---

# EASTER – A FRESH START

**1**  Easter – the festival which celebrates the resurrection of Jesus Christ from the dead.

**2**  Put to death by Crucifixion on Good Friday.

Good Friday = Holy Friday

**3**  The day before is Maundy Thursday (from Latin *Mandatum* = Command).

It was that day that Jesus gave a New Commandment:

'I give you a New Commandment: Love one another.'

**4**  On the third day after Good Friday – Easter Sunday – Jesus rose from the dead.

Listen to the story:

St Mark Chapter 16, verses 1–8.

**5**  Easter is the happiest festival of the year.

**6**  Time when everything comes to life:

Churches decorated with flowers
New Easter Bonnet – or shoes

7    Easter Egg – now chocolate – once real eggs – symbol of resurrection.

8    Like Christmas, Easter celebrations go back long before the Christianity.

       The Anglo Saxon word EOSTRE = THE GODDESS OF SPRING.

9    The old Pagan Spring customs became the symbols of the Christian Easter, rejoicing at the bursting forth of nature in the Spring. Were transferred to Christian joy at Easter.

10    For the Christian the rising of Jesus from death means:

           Death is not the end
           God is all-powerful
           Jesus is the Son of God.

**PRAYER**

O God, we give thanks for the death and resurrection of Jesus and the hope of eternal life which these events have brought us.

Help us this Eastertide to understand more fully how Jesus came into the world in order to demonstrate your love and reveal your care and concern for all.

---

NOTES – EASTER-A FRESH START

---

# EASTER – THE FISH

1    Easter to most represents end of weariness and cold of winter.

2    Spring begins officially on March 21st

       But 'March winds, April showers, bring forth May flowers.'

3    It can seem a long time to Easter.

4    For Christianity Easter represents much more.

**5** GCSE question recently:

'Which do you think is more important, Christmas or Easter? Give reasons.'

**6** As in all questions of this type both could be right – as long as you have given your reasons.

**7** Christmas – Birth of Jesus
  Promised Messiah
  Son of God
  God in human flesh.

**8** If all this is true – what a wonderful event.

**9** Some would argue (logically):

If Jesus had not been born, there would have been no Easter.

**10** But Christianity did not begin at Jesus' birth.

It began when his followers claimed he had risen from the dead.

**11** Listen to the story:

St Luke, Chapter 24, verses 13–34.

**12** It was then that Christianity spread like a bushfire throughout the known world.

**13** Christians were persecuted for a long time by the Romans so when Christians met one another they had a secret sign:

A Fish

**14** They would draw it with the end of their staff in the sand or soil.

**15** The Greek for Fish is IXTHUS.

| | |
|---|---|
| I | = Jesus |
| X | = Christ |
| THEOU | = of God |
| HUIOS | = Son |
| SOTER | = Saviour. |

**16** This sums up the Christian Faith.

**17** Without the death and resurrection of Jesus the Christian beliefs represented by the Fish would not be possible.

**PRAYER**

O God, The Father of our Lord Jesus Christ, who was born at Christmastide, died on Good Friday and rose from the grave on Easter Sunday, teach us to understand the promise of Christmas, the sorrow of Holy Week and the joy of Easter.

# ANXIETY

1   Read St. Matthew, Chapter 6, verses 25–34.

2   Stress and anxiety – the disease of our time.
    It affects young and old.
    Heart disease is at an alarming level.

3   Much of it is caused by the pace and complexity of modern life.

4   Psychological illness much more difficult to cure.
    People say: 'Pull yourself together.' But you cannot.

5   Many religions have taught people to cope with stress:
    Buddha, Jesus, Yoga (Hinduism).

6   Today I have quoted from Jesus:
    'Do not worry about tomorrow.'
    Each day has enough troubles of its own.

7   Some people have taken that to mean:
    Never think about the future: never plan for the future.

8   How ridiculous! How could we survive without planning and providing for
    tomorrow, next year, old age, etc.'

9   What Jesus was saying was:
    Do not be anxious.

10   We worry so much about the future *but so often the fears are unfounded.*

11   Take interviews, exams, illness – our worst fears rarely materialise.

12   But even if they do, things will be much worse if we worry beforehand.

13   Again, this does not mean do not prepare. It means remain calm.

14   Religion is often a help to a large number of people to cope with fear, loneliness, illness, death.

15   The answer is: peace of mind.

16   How do you get it?
     (i) Relaxation.
     (ii) Recreation = Re-creation
     (iii) Talking to others.
         Someone to confide in – a Friend, a Doctor, a Teacher.
     (iv) Helping others particularly those worse off than ourselves.
     (v) Faith in God.

**PRAYER**

We ask that strain and stress may be removed from our lives and that we may be given a calm mind and a peaceful spirit.

---

NOTES – ANXIETY

---

# SIKHISM – BAISAKHI

1   Also spelt – Vaisakhi.

(a) N. Indian Harvest Festival celebrated in Spring.
(b) New Year's Day in N. Punjab (usually falls on 13th April).
(c) Guru Nanak – founder of Sikhism – started missionary travels.

2   But at Baisakhi of 1699 Guru Gobind Singh made it the birthday of Sikhs.

3   The Guru commanded followers to gather at Anandpur for morning prayer.

Over a hundred thousand there.

4   After Prayers, Guru addressed congregation, then drew sword and asked for a volunteer to die for his faith.

5   One volunteered. Taken into tent. Guru appeared with blood-stained sword and called for others.

6   5 volunteered – later produced alive (really blood of animal).

7   The Guru baptised the five with special nectar prepared in steel bowl to which wife added sugar crystals.

Mixture stirred by 'Khanda' – double-edged sword.

Later the Guru asked the 5 to baptise him.

8   Thus was born the 'Khalsa'

– The Brotherhood – The Pure Ones.

9   The Khalsa 'Code of Conduct' known as the 5 'Ks':

    (i)  Kes – uncut hair
    (ii)  Kanga – comb
    (iii) Kara – steel bangle
    (iv) Kachahara – sewn shorts
    (v)  Kirpan – small dagger.

10  The men took the name Singh = Lion
    The women took name Kaur = Princess.

11  On Baisakhi great festivities round Golden Temple (Darbar Sahib).

    (a) Continuous reading of Guru Granth Sahib (Holy Book).
    (b) 5 men wearing yellow turbans and robes – represent 5 'Brothers.'
    (c) Thousands fed in Temple kitchen (meal = Langar).
    (d) New members admitted.
    (e) Presents given, turbans exchanged.
    (f)  New clothes.
    (g) Family gatherings.

12  Should remember with sadness that on Baisakhi Day 1919 at Jallianwala Bagh, General Dyer, Commissioner of Amritsar, ordered his troops to fire on a large crowd of men, women and children, as he considered it a political meeting.

**PRAYER**

A Sikh Prayer

O True God, one, to whom you give, shall receive the same.

He will constantly go on singing your praises and glories and will fix your name in his heart.

NOTES – SIKHISM - BAISAKHI

# SIKHISM – BIRTHDAY OF GURU NANAK

1   Guru Nanak (1469–1539) was Founder of Sikh religion.

First Guru followed by 8 others.

2   Born in Talwani, now called Nankana Sahib in Pakistan.

3   Date of Birthday varies each year (follows Lunar Month, not calendar) but usually in November.

4   Celebrations last 3 days – the third being the birthday.

*Day 1*: At Gurdwara (Temple) with continuous recitation of Guru Granth (Holy Book) 1430 pages; takes approximately 48 hours to read.

*Day 2*: (In India) Procession with 5 Sikhs dressed as original Khalsa with the Holy Book carried behind them. Singers, Swordsmen, Gymnastics, Wrestling, Preaching.

*Day 3*: (Actual Birthday) Prayer meeting starts about 4.00 a.m. Singing of hymns followed by prayers, speeches, recitations, discourses on life and teaching of Guru Nanak.

After final prayer, holy pudding (Karah Parsad) is distributed and food (Langar) is served to all.

**5** Sometimes on third day a night-long Prayer Vigil is held.

Praises of Guru sung until actual time of his birth (approximately 1.20 a.m.).

**6** All religions have their sacred stories about their leader.

**7** In Sikhism there is the story of Guru Nanak and the Carpet.

Guru Nanak loved by all: rich, poor, old, young.

People liked to show love and respect by giving presents. These could be very small or very expensive.

Nanak did not keep gifts. Helped other people with them.

One day, a Carpet Weaver made up mind to give the Guru the finest present he could – best carpet he had ever made. Guru would be able to sit on this, he thought.

Carpet took months. When completed, weaver unrolled it and said:

'Honour me, my Master, by sitting on my carpet.'

Guru said:

'Nature's carpet – the grass – is good enough for me. Please put carpet to good use for me. See that dog over there with puppies dying of cold and hunger. Put carpet over them and give them food and milk. It would make me happy to save them from suffering.'

So the weaver did as the Guru requested and this gave them both much happiness.

**PRAYER**

(Words of Guru Nanak)

O God, may I serve you in my childhood and contemplate on you in my youth and old age.

---

NOTES – SIKHISM-BIRTHDAY OF GURU NANAK

# MAY DAY

1   The first day of May, traditionally May Day.

2   This holiday has only been revived in the last few years in this country but it is actually the oldest holiday.

3   It goes back to Roman times –

Goddess Flora – of Flowers –

and beyond to Pagan times.

4   May Day was highlight of year. People celebrating passing of winter and new life of springtime.

5   In past day began very early.

Young people went to woods to gather branches and flowers.

Young women washed faces in early dew – for complexion and against illnesses.

6   Villages arranged processions with people carrying boughs of sycamore and hawthorn.

7   Pride of place given to young tree to be set up as maypole.

8   *Maypole* – decorated with flowers and ribbons. Later in day, people danced round it. Lively tune. Long coloured ribbons plaited, people reversed and ribbons unplaited.

9   *Queen of May* – greatest honour for young woman to be made 'Queen' – the prettiest – presided over day's activities.

10   *Green Man or Jack in the Green* – a man covered by a 'cage' of leaves.

11   There was stamping and ringing of bells to wake up spirit of ground after winter and drive out evil spirits.

12   At end of day fires were lit, people danced, there were contests and maybe a roasted ox.

13   May Day celebrations did not find favour with Church.

Oliver Cromwell forbade them.

Revived under Charles II.

14   Spring is a time for hope. Looking forward to Summer.

15   May considered a beautiful month. Old rhyme:

March winds and April Showers

Bring forth May flowers.

**16** Wonderful to watch Nature through changing scenes.

Winter          – all seeds dead
Spring          – sprouts and buds
May into Summer – full blossom, full fruit.

**PRAYER**

We rejoice in the beauty of nature and marvel at the changing seasons which together bring rest, renewal and revival to Mother Earth.

---

NOTES – MAY DAY

---

# SPEAKING "PROPERLY"

**1** People may have said to you:

'Why don't you speak properly?'

**2** What do they mean? and what does it matter?

**3** Sometimes people criticise our speech because it is slovenly and careless.

**4** In education we try to teach people to do everything to the highest standards.

**5** This includes speaking.

**6** Interesting – in recent years there has been a re-think on making people speak 'BBC' or Queen's/King's English.

**7** Dialects and regional accents should be encouraged and even incorporated in oral and written English.

**8** The power of speech is a wonderful human faculty. To be dumb is a dreadful handicap.

**9** We can confer and plan and send messages and record our voices for others to listen to either now or in the future.

**10** No one would disagree, I am sure, on how important speech is:

(a) To communicate e.g. 999 call.
(b) To converse.
(c) To indicate feelings, ideas.
(d) To persuade, argue one's case.
(e) To entertain.
(f) To teach,

and so on.

**11** What is then to speak 'properly?'

**12** Firstly it is to use language that is appropriate for the occasion.

Are you speaking to: A friend?
                     The boss?
                     Parents?
                     Examiner?

**13** Many employers say they reject applicants because of their speech. They say, for example, that unless employees can be clearly understood on the telephone they are of no use.

**14** Secondly then, speaking 'properly' means 'being understood.'

**15** Thirdly, remember bad language offends and shocks many people. They have a right to expect you not to use it in their presence.

**16** Speaking can become an art or a professional asset:

eg Politician, Actor, Clergyman.

**17** (Use if appropriate). To finish, let me tell you what the judges look for in a 'Youth Speaks' competition:

The discipline of the logical sequence,
Clarity,
Confidence,
Entertainment.

**18** So often human beings have believed God has spoken – either to individuals or nations.

**19** Perhaps, the power to speak is God's unique gift to humans who can communicate with him by spoken or silent prayer.

**PRAYER**

We give thanks for the power of speech. May we learn to use this gift wisely, correctly and for the good of ourselves and others and may we show compassion to those who cannot speak or suffer from a speech impediment.

---

NOTES – SPEAKING "PROPERLY"

---

# SPORTS DAY/ATHLETICS

1  Sports Day/Athletics – (recent or coming event).

2  Most natural things for us to do are:

    run, jump and throw.

3  Really sports just consist of that.

4  Do you have to be specially built?
   Not really.

5  Look at sportsmen and women:
   All shapes and sizes.

6  Of course build can help.
   Like brains. Can give unfair advantage.

7  But look at a group of runners and you will see a very mixed bag.

8  If you are very big, perhaps you will shine at the Shot or Tug-O-War.

**9** The secret of the great sportsman or woman is:

> Fitness of Body
> +
> Fitness of Mind.

**10** The Ancient Romans who were very keen on fitness would have said:

> 'Mens sana in corpore sano.'
> (A healthy mind in a healthy body).

**11** To succeed in sport one needs:

(a) Training – hours and hours.
(b) Determination.
(c) Willingness to push oneself beyond one's previous best.
(d) Competitiveness.

**12** Many famous people have likened Life to a race.

**13** St Paul says:

'Let us strip off every weight and the sin which clings to us and run with patience the race that is set before us.'

HEBREW 12.1

**14** In life:

(a) There is a tape to run to.
(b) We need fitness and determination.
(c) We must have strict control of ourselves.
(d) We must learn competitiveness.

**15** In the end the important thing is not to win but to have given of our best.

**PRAYER**

Help us to make ourselves the fittest possible for the race of life. Teach us not to be concerned only with winning but with giving the very best we have.

---

NOTES – SPORTS DAY / ATHLETICS

---

# ANOTHER DIMENSION TO LIFE

(Based on the book: *Jonathan Livingston Seagull*, by Richard Bach)

1   This book is a story of a Seagull.

But no ordinary Seagull. For him it was not eating that mattered, but flying.

'Why is it so hard to be like the rest of the flock, Son?' his mother asked.

2   But Jonathan thought it was a waste of time just searching for food. He wanted to study flight. He sought a world record.

3   He dived from a thousand feet, two thousand feet, passed 70 m.p.h. Reached 90 m.p.h., then disaster struck. He could not pull out and smashed down into a brick-hard sea.

4   After this he decided to return to the flock.

'There's no way round it,' he said, 'I am a Seagull,'

5   Then he thought of the Falcon and its tiny, short wings.

'That's the answer,' he said to himself. 'I must fold most of my wings and just fly on the tips'.

6   Then came success. Five thousand feet up and he swooped down at 240 m.p.h.

'The speed was power and the speed was joy and the speed was beauty.'

7   When the flock hears of this 240 m.p.h., he thought, they will be wild with joy. There is so much more to living, there is a reason for life.

No more ignorance, but creatures of excellence and intelligence and skill.

8   But when Jonathan landed the gulls were gathered in Council.

9   'Stand to the centre' they ordered. This was only demanded in cases of shame and dishonour.

'Jonathan stand to the centre for reckless irresponsibility. One day you will learn that irresponsibility does not pay.'

10   He was to be banished from Gull society to a solitary cliff.

11   His protests fell on deaf ears. 'Who is more responsible than a gull who finds and follows a meaning, a higher purpose in life?'

12   The story is a kind of parable.

The world is not very tolerant of those who:

>Rise above the ordinary,
>Dream or see visions,
>Have found a new meaning to life,
>Are not interested in money or goods.

**13** Martin Luther King had a Dream . . . he was assassinated.

**14** History is littered with stories of those persecuted, decapitated, hanged, burned, crucified, because they wanted to lift people above their ordinary, hum-drum, meaningless lives.

**PRAYER**

Let us thank God there are still people in the world who see purpose, meaning and another dimension to life, people who lead us to God.

---

NOTES – ANOTHER DIMENSION TO LIFE

---

# STEREOTYPING (SEXISM)

**1** Some years ago there was a television advertisement which began with : 'What is a Mum?'

**2** It went on to describe all the things mothers do for us.

**3** It finished with an advertisement for what the advertisers claimed was the best washing powder.

**4** For advertisements there is often very narrow stereotyping:

MUMS: Wash clothes
Cook
Wash dishes
Clean
Vacuum
Feed
Look after baby
Shop
Iron etc.

DADS: Go to work
Decorate
Mend cars
Do house repairs
Play darts
Drink beer
Go to football matches
Smoke cigarettes/cigars etc.

**5** The trouble is: that is how many of us have been brought up:

GIRLS: Play with dolls
Wear pretty clothes
Help in the house
Sew and knit

BOYS: Play with trains or computers
Play rough games
Go to football matches
Repair bicycles
Learn about cars.

**6** This is what is called: Sexism.

The stereotyping of girls
of boys.

**7** Of course there are obvious physical differences and only women can have babies.

**8** But the truth is that we are all a bit of a mixture.

There is a bit of the boy and girl in all of us.

**9** Sometimes there can be more of the girl in a boy or vice-versa.

**10** Neither sex is inferior.

Both are equal.

**11** And there are no defined barriers except the ones we make.

**12** Why shouldn't: A girl be a motor mechanic?

A boy be a dress designer?
Boys clean the house and wash up?
Girls build their own bicycle or have a toy train?

13   Similarly in Schools: there is no such thing as 'Girls' subjects or 'Boys' subjects.

14   Our minds are brainwashed by society so that some people think boys can be 'cissy' and girls can be 'butch.'

15   It is our job to help you stop thinking like that.

16   What is a Mum?
There is a bit of Mum in all of us.

**PRAYER**

Help us to remember that we are all equal. Give us tolerance and understanding of those who are different from others and guard us from ever thinking of anyone as inferior.

```
NOTES – STEREOTYPING (SEXISM)




```

# MEDICAL SERVICES

1   We so often take medical services for granted.

   Telephone: doctor, ambulance
   Visit or stay in hospital.

2   There are always grumbles about the National Health Service. These are frequently justified.

3   Some would argue that the National Health Service is deteriorating rapidly:

   Waiting lists
   Closures
   Lack of night-duty doctors.

4   Others would say that more and more money is being poured in but the demands on the National Health Service outstrip the resources.

5   But elsewhere in the world things are very different.

6   Take India, Africa, South America as examples.

7   Or even the Australian 'Outback' which is mainly a hot, dry area of plains and deserts with small towns and homesteads dotted about.

8   A young Australian Clergyman called John Flynn decided in 1912 to go to the Outback.

9   He wanted to help people in these isolated areas.

10  He was already a member of the Inland Mission, which had clinics and he had some medical knowledge.

11  But these clinics and his knowledge were not enough in an emergency.

12  Moreover he and his friends travelled mainly on horseback.

13  What could he do to improve the situation?

14  The first advance was when an electrical engineer produced a pedal radio. This generated its own electricity.

15  Through this invention, John Flynn was able to set up the first radio base in Australia in 1928.

16  Things then really began to move:
    (a) Pedal radios were distributed.
    (b) A Doctor was employed.
    (c) An Aeroplane was hired.

17  The first patient was treated by a 'Flying Doctor', as they came to be called, was on the 15th May, 1928.

18  Nowadays Australians in the Outback take it for granted that the 'Flying Doctor' service is available.

19  Thousands are helped every year.

    Some are visited, many more radio for advice.

20  In 1951 John Flynn died, famous for starting an outstanding medical service: 'The *Royal* Flying Doctor Service'.

    **PRAYER**

    We are indebted to all those who deal with the sick, the injured and the wounded.

We recognise with gratitude the skill and patience of those who seek cures for the terrible diseases which afflict the body and the mind.

We pray that those who suffer may find comfort and those who nurse may show compassion.

NOTES – MEDICAL SERVICES

# WHO IS MY NEIGHBOUR?

1   Read the story of the Good Samaritan.

    (St Luke, Chapter 10 verses 30–37, preferably in a modern version).

2   Jesus told this story partly to show up the hypocrisy of the religious people of his day.

3   The priest and the temple worker (Levite) 'passed by' and did nothing.

4   The Samaritan was despised by orthodox Jews. In fact it was common for a Jew to spit on the ground when he passed a Samaritan.

5   The historical reason for this attitude was that the Samaritans were Jews who had inter-married with other tribes and were therefore not pure Jewish blood.

6   Who is my neighbour?

    The answer is anybody in need.

7   They may actually live next door.

8   Sometimes we are so keen to help those in need abroad that we forget the people in our street or town.

9  It is also a fact that it is easier to give money to charity than actually do something practical.

10  Of course, aid for Third World countries is absolutely vital. How can we let people starve if we can stop it?

11  There has been wonderful support for needy countries, e.g. Band Aid, Sport Aid etc.

12  In the story of the Good Samaritan, practical help is given as well as money. He even promises to come back later to see how the victim is.

13  What are we going to do to help those in need around us?

　(i) The old – be observant e.g. milk on doorstep.
　(ii) Offering to do little jobs e.g. gardening, shopping, changing library books.
　(iii) Simply being kind and considerate.
　(iv) Adopting an old person or a harrassed young mother.

14  Look around – see if you can make a personal contribution to the life of this community around us.

15  Or see if there are projects already set up that you can join in with.

16  Like the Samaritan, you do not have to possess special talents.

Just be kind, thoughtful, compassionate.

**PRAYER**

Let us be kind and considerate, on the look out for signs of trouble in our neighbourhood and to be ready to help wherever we are needed.

NOTES – WHO IS MY NEIGHBOUR?

# DEAFNESS

1   Can everybody hear me?

2   In a hall one needs to raise one's voice.

3   But we have two ears so that we can hear everything in stereo.
    (It took humans ages to realise you need two speakers).

4   Some people do not have the benefit of hearing in both ears. They are partially deaf.

5   (The school nurse says) some of our pupils suffer from partial deafness.

6   Some people are born deaf. Some will go deaf.

7   Danger of going deaf later in life as a result of excessive pop music.
    (Too many decibels).

8   But it could also happen as a result of virus or accident.

9   Deafness gets very little sympathy.

10  Blindness – yes. Everybody rushes to help. The white stick or 'Guide Dog' alert us to the problem.

11  The deaf have no sign – except perhaps the hearing aid.

12  Deaf often teased. People lose patience with Granny and Grandad.

13  But many deaf people have bravely fought against the handicap.

14  A good example is:
    Jack Ashley, M.P.

15  Born in 1920 of poor family, left school to become a labourer.

16  At age 22, a Trade Union Official and youngest member of Borough Council.
    At age 24, Scholarship to Ruskin College, Oxford.

17  In 1966 elected M.P. for Stoke-on-Trent, South.
    Set for brilliant career.
    Then disaster struck.
    Caught a virus infection. Left him totally deaf.

18  Learnt to lip read but returned to a totally silent House of Commons.

**19** Was only totally deaf M.P. of any Parliament in the world.

**20** Became known as 'The Champion of the Disabled.'

**PRAYER**

We give thanks for the gift of hearing. We remember the deaf and the partially deaf.

We ask for sympathy for those who are hard of hearing.

---

NOTES – DEAFNESS

---

# LISTENING

**1** Lots of people hear, not everybody listens.

There is a difference.

**2** Listening is a skill. It takes thought and concentration.

**3** The world is desperately short of good listeners.

Plenty of good thinkers.

**4** Listening has been greatly assisted by the invention of the telephone.

**5** Alexander Graham Bell invented the telephone but he was really looking for a machine to help the deaf.

**6** He set up a school to train teachers of deaf and he experimented with idea of sending speech by electricity.

**7** The telephone has been a boon to so many people.

Someone (even a recorded voice) at the other end to listen to you.

**8** Look in any paper and you will see somewhere an advertisement from the Samaritans:

'Desperate? Need Help? Ring . . .'

**9** Rev. Chad Varah started the Samaritan service on the 2nd November 1953. How could people with problems find help?

**10** He was appointed Rector of St Stephens Walbrook, in the heart of London. Became headquarters of the Samaritans.

**11** Ring the Samaritans and a voice answers:

'Can I help you?'

**12** Call may last long time or caller may be persuaded to meet the Duty Samaritan at local headquarters.

**13** The calls each year reach millions in number.

**14** All staffed by volunteers who give up their time to help.

**15** An appropriate name: Samaritan.
Someone who: Cares
     Listens
     Helps

**16** All of us need someone at some time who will listen to us.

**17** If you are not a good talker, why not develop the skill of listening.

**18** Experts tell us there are more and more lonely people who would love to talk to someone.

**19** A good listener can be of more value than a good talker.

**20** That is why I linked listening and the telephone.

**21** To many the telephone is a life-line.

**22** There is also prayer. God is always listening and we can pray whatever the time, whatever the place.

**PRAYER**

In The Silence:
Let us remember those who are lonely, depressed, sad, suicidal.

If there is someone we know personally let us pray for them now.

(*Pause*)

We pray for God's blessing on all who try to help and particularly the Samaritans.

# THE BAOBAB TREE

1   Baobab tree everywhere in Central Africa.

Huge, gnarled trunks, stubby twisted branches, grey in colour.

2   Give no shade from sun except few weeks after rains. They produce leaves and store up water in hollow trunks.

3   Africans would never uproot Baobab Tree:
   (i) Collects water and keeps it during dry weather.
   (ii) If water not used, seeps into roots and stops erosion of soil.
   (iii) Encourages growth of green grass.
   (iv) Roots grip firmly and stop soil cracking.
   (v) When trunk is empty it is very cool, natural fridge for storage of meat.

4   Belief of Africans that God will stop rains falling if a Baobab tree is dug up or moved.

5   Westerners thought this was nonsense, so shortly after War, Britain decided to grow ground-nuts in Tanganyika, modern Tanzania. (Ground-nut is another name for peanut or monkey-nut).

6   Vast sums of money allocated. Thousands of civil servants employed.

7   First the ground had to be cleared. Fleets of tractors to clear scrub.
   *But* ground dotted with Baobab trees.

8   Local people pleaded with workmen not to touch these trees, to no avail.

9   Bulldozer blades broke; Tractor tracks stripped. Then explosives used.

10  Finally ground cleared, thousands of ground-nut plants put in.

**11** Western experts said: 'When rains come, they will sprout, and flourish. All S. Tanganyika will benefit.'

**12** But rains did not come, 'Never mind next year.' – Next year – no rains. Third year – almost no rain.

**13** So area declared unfit for ground-nuts.

**14** LESSONS:
  (i) Humans must pay attention to natural vegetation and balance of nature.
 (ii) Trees, in particular have important place in nature.
(iii) Many believe God created this wonderful world. There is danger of Humans destroying their planet by unthinking actions.

**PRAYER**

We rejoice in the wonders of Nature: the sun of summer, the cold of winter, the rain bringing fertility and growth, the fields, the sea, the sky. But particularly we give thanks for trees which beautify the countryside and provide so many benefits for the rest of Nature.

---

NOTES – THE BAOBAB TREE

---

# HARVEST IN THE CITY

**1** A favourite Harvest hymn is:

'Come ye thankful people come
Raise the song of Harvest home.'

**2** But is this relevant in the city?

**3** Thank God for:

      Electric Razors
      Cars
      Colour Televisions.

4    There is a new Harvest:

The Harvest of the silicon chip. (Silicon, next to Oxygen, biggest elementary constituent of Earth's crust).

5    In the city we do not have direct contact with the crop-growing process.

6    Yet we try to celebrate Harvest in the traditional way:

        Fruit, vegetables, corn, Harvest loaf.

7    Of course, we could not live without the farming of the land.

8    We must also remember the Harvest of the Sea.

9    What would we do without basic things like water – which we take so much for granted?

10    But God is not just the God of the soil and sea.

He is the God of Machinery
            Technology
            Electronics
            Computerisation.

11    The Hymn which is relevant to Harvest in the City is:

        God of concrete, God of steel,
        God of piston and of wheel,
        God of pylon, God of steam,
        God of girder and of beam,
        God of atom, God of mine
        All the world of power is thine!

12    We should thank God for *all* the wonders of this world.

13    This includes the things that make our lives so much more comfortable:

        Microwave Ovens
        Dishwashers
        Video Recorders
        Washing Machines
        Personal Stereos
        Computers.

14    Let us also thank God for fast transport, for supermarkets and motorways.

15    We must realise that everything that we discover was put there by God to be discovered.

'Come ye thankful people come.'

**PRAYER**

We give thanks for the wonderful things there are in our world for us to discover. May we be given the intelligence to explore all this earth's possibilities, and show our gratitude for all the benefits we enjoy.

---

NOTES – HARVEST IN THE CITY

---

# HARVEST FESTIVAL

1  We sometimes sing (have sung) the hymn: 'Now Thank we all our God.'

2  It is important to say 'Thank You.'

   We do not always remember – to anybody, but particularly to God.

3  Take so much for granted. Everything comes to us so easily.

4  We never go short.

   If we run out, we go down to shops – always full, nearly always open.

5  What kind of harvest have we had?

   I do not suppose you know. You probably do not care. It does not affect us really.

6  If home-grown food is short, we buy foreign goods. Perhaps a few pence dearer sometimes when in short supply – but we do not mind.

7  We hear of: milk lakes, butter mountains, but does it really sink in?

   Why cannot they give it away to the poor and starving? (Sometimes cheap E.E.C. butter sold to poor).

8  So has it been a bad year? If potatoes, beans are short we will buy tins instead.

9  We talk sometimes about going hungry – but we do not know what it means.

10  Just look at the pictures of starving in Africa or India.

Bones sticking out, stomach swollen, covered in flies.

11  When have we been like that?

12  But 200 years ago even in this country, if your harvest failed you starved.

13  People believed there were spirits in the soil, which made crops grow.

14  This is the reason for Corn Dollies, pieces of corn tied together to resemble a figure, mostly a woman. Believed spirit would stay in Dolly until next Spring when spirit would return to corn.

15  No longer believe in such spirits but can understand superstitions in other parts of world where everybody depends on rains.

If they do not come – disaster.

16  Are we thankful?

Then let us show it by giving generously to others who suffer from famine and poverty.

**PRAYER**

We express our grateful thanks for the harvest of field, orchard and sea. Let us not take these blessings for granted but be mindful of the sufferings and deprivations of people in other parts of the world.

NOTES – HARVEST FESTIVAL

# WORKING TOGETHER

1  One of Aesop's Fables tells of two men walking along a road and finding an axe lying on ground. They are friends but man who saw it said:

'*I have* found an Axe. That will be useful.'

'Don't say *I*' says second man, 'say *we* have found an Axe. We are friends on road together. Surely it is *our* Axe and we shall sell it and share money.'

Second man would not agree.

Not gone far when owner of Axe came running towards them. Moment he saw first man carrying Axe he threatened to prosecute him.

'Oh dear!' cried the first man, 'we are in trouble.'

'Don't say *we*' said second man, 'say rather *you* are in trouble. You would not let me share the prize, you can hardly expect me to share the trouble.'

2   There is far too much 'I', 'I', 'I', and 'mine.'

Too self-centred, selfish.

3   Need to think of others, share with others. This is what we would like you to do here in School.

### All Working Together

4   Otherwise there is no community and school *is* a community.

5   What we do affects others.

Making a contribution to school life.

Thinking of the good of community.

6   Not only 'in' school but 'on way' too.

People outside judge whole school by the actions of a few individuals.

7   Pupils sometimes say what has it got to do with anybody else?

The answer is everything – because they are pupils and they represent school.

8   Going back to Fable of Axe, we can be so selfish, particularly when things are going well.

9   Then when things go wrong we expect others to help us.

10   None of us is self-sufficient. We all need friends.

Old saying: 'A friend in need is a friend indeed.'

11   We can only have friends if we are friendly too. It is a two-way process.

12   That means we have to help others when they are in trouble even if everything at the time is alright for us.

### PRAYER

We ask that we may learn to be less selfish and more thoughtful of others. Let us use 'I' sparingly and remember that often we need to work together. May we not only enjoy the friendship of others but show friendship ourselves.

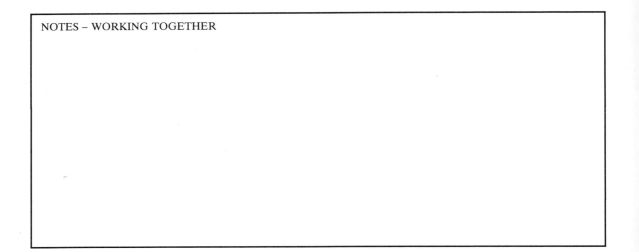

# IMMIGRATION

1   Sometimes tempted to think that immigration only affects this country.

2   In fact, people have travelled to new countries throughout history.

3   The problem of being accepted is also not new. Natives of many lands have resented and fought the newcomers.

4   A wonderful story comes from Persia (now Iran) a long time ago.

    A group of people who worshipped the God Zoroaster were despised because of their religion.

    Decided to leave Persia for India.

    Eventually, after difficult journey, arrived in India at a place called Sanjan on coast of Gujurat.

    The ruler was called The Rana.

5   The travellers sent a message to The Rana saying 'Please can we settle in your country, we've travelled far to get here?'

6   The only reply they received was a bowl of milk – *full to the brim*.

7   The mesage was clear – 'Full Up.'

8   But the Persians did not give up. They thought of an answer. They poured sugar into bowl. Sugar dissolved, milk became sweet but did not overflow.

9   The bowl was returned to The Rana, who was pleased and allowed them to stay.

10  The group, known as Parsees, still exist in India today.

**11** There is an important lesson for us in this story.

Let us think of Britain as that bowl of milk. The sugar sweetened it but did not make it overflow.

**12** If you study the number of immigrants coming into this country, it is minute compared with our population. 4%· of total population in recent figures.

It will not make us overflow.

**13** Also, the immigrants have a great deal to offer.

Let us stop thinking of them as problems. They are assets.

**14** They bring with them rich cultures: language, literature, music, which will sweeten our culture.

**15** And if you say 'But we want to stay British,' what does that mean?

**16** The British are a mixture of many races who have settled here over the centuries.

Who can claim to be pure English?

**17** And what about the U.S.A. or Australia? Are the inhabitants any worse for being immigrants?

**18** Every country has been 'infiltrated' at one time or other.

**19** Let us think positively about enrichment rather than problems.

**PRAYER**

We pray for greater understanding of those who are of a different race, colour or creed from our own. May we welcome them to our community and learn to appreciate the good that they bring with them.

NOTES – IMMIGRATION

# "THE GRASS ON THE OTHER SIDE . . . . ."

1   There is a lovely story of a boy who lived on top of a hill.

Each morning looked out of window over valley to hill on other side. On this hill was a house which had golden windows.

He longed to see house. He wished he lived there rather than here.

One morning he made up mind. I'm going to see house for myself. Set off early but the journey much longer than expected. When finally came up other hillside it was getting dark. Imagine his disappointment when he saw the windows were not golden but just like his.

Too late to go back, knocked on door. Little old lady answered. Told his story. The old lady welcomed him in, introduced to husband, gave him supper and put him to bed.

In morning woke up to glorious sunshine. Looked out of window across valley to his house. Guess what? Yes, you are right. His house had golden windows.

He was glad to get home to his own, lovely house.

2   Easy to think what others have is better:

      House, family, looks, brains.

3   There is an old saying:

      'The grass on the other side is always greener.'

4   But it is a question of how you look at it.

5   Your friends are probably envying you.

6   Of course, does not mean we should never try to improve ourselves.

      To do better
      To be better
      To get better things.

7   Man only survived because improved himself.

8   But real secret of life is to make best of what you have:

      Your brains,
      Your looks,
      Your family.

9   Many times we do not realise how much we have.

**10** Sadly it is often only when we lose something, or more importantly, someone, we realise how much we miss them.

**PRAYER**

We look for help not only to be content with what we have but to be able to use it to the best advantage, at the same time always seeking to improve ourselves.

---

NOTES – "THE GRASS ON THE OTHER SIDE . . . ."

---

# BEETHOVEN'S MASS IN D

**1** What is your favourite music? Why?

Is it the singer or the group?

Or a particular type of music?

**2** 'Pop' music suggests literally that some music is more popular than others.

The strange thing is that the 'Pop' music of today can become the old-fashioned music of tomorrow.

**3** If 'Pop' is very good, it can in time become a classic:

eg The Beatles' music.

**4** I expect you have heard of the great composer Ludwig van Beethoven (1770–1827).

A 'Pop' composer in his day. Now regarded as classical, although still popular.

**5** Beethoven wrote the 'Mass in D.'

Probably greatest music he ever wrote. Music to accompany the Holy Eucharist.

**6** Sometimes music lifts you right out of yourself.

Soul seems to come out of body.

Whole being is taken over.

**7** The 'Mass in D' has that kind of effect on many people.

They feel they are transported to heaven.

**8** I am going to play you some of that wonderful music now.

(*Having first arranged this with the Media Resources Officer, there is, in fact, no music but silence.*)

**9** (*Try to wait a couple of minutes, although the pupils will begin to shout out 'it is not on' 'we cannot here it,' etc.*

*Keep them going by saying 'Shh!' and 'you'll have to listen carefully because it has a very quiet beginning.'*).

**10** Did you hear it? (wait).

No, of course you did not because I did not play it.

**11** But say I had and you did not hear it.

**12** Beethoven wrote Mass in D when he was totally deaf.

(He went deaf aged 30).

He composed it all in his head. He never heard it.

**13** First performed May 1824 in Vienna, conducted it himself.

**14** Did not know they were clapping at end until the Contralto singer turned him round, to face audience.

**15** The Mass is sometimes used in concerts by the Royal National Institute for Deaf.

**16** Be sympathetic to the terrible handicap of deafness.

## PRAYER

We give thanks for all our gifts but particularly today for the gift of hearing, for music, for the sounds of nature and wildlife, for the voices of family and friends.

Let us show greater understanding with those who cannot hear, and have patience to bear with them.

NOTES – BEETHOVEN'S MASS IN D

# THE SCHOOL COMMUNITY

1   Human beings are gregarious, (based on Latin word *Grex* = A herd), the herd instinct.

It means we need one another.

2   It is very difficult to live alone. Some do – exceptional – hermits, holy men/women.

3   We could learn on own – by correspondence course, private tutor.

4   Most of us would miss other people.

Inter-action – we learn from one another but also enjoy other people's company.

5   But there are difficulties – particularly if numbers are large.

Look at dangers of large crowds. If no control or if people do not show consideration and thoughtfulness for others.

6   In large crowds, more needed than just consideration. There has to be law and order to ensure safety, security, peace of mind.

7   Schools contain large numbers.

Sometimes during day masses of people entering, leaving building or milling about in playground or gathering in hall.

8   It is a wonderful feeling to belong. Feel part of an organisation, a community.

9   With belonging, one needs to give as well as take.

The community will only be at its best if everybody in it makes a positive contribution.

10   Unfortunately that is idealistic. Some members are apathetic, a few are destructive.

11   So every community, including a school, has to ensure smooth running and also protect itself.

12   It does this by having rules.

13   Think of the roads. Where would we be without rule of driving on left (or right in some countries) or traffic lights?

14   So in school:

(a) Some rules are for safety:
   no running, walk on left.
(b) Some are for work and good order:
   noise, classroom order.
(c) Some are training for adult life:
   good manners, punctuality, attendance, appearance.

**15**  So when people come into school they judge us by those standards.

**16**  Some pupils say: 'I can't wait to leave school and rules behind me.'

**17**  What nonsense! The rules out there can be much tougher.

You try being late, or dressing badly or being rude when you are at work.

You will just get your cards.

**18**  Do not imagine rules just apply here, they are the basis of every community.

**PRAYER**

We value the company of other people and the benefits that come from living in a community.

May we learn to take our share of responsibility towards others and to understand the problems of loneliness and isolation.

---

NOTES – THE SCHOOL COMMUNITY

---

# WHAT ARE WE WORTH?

**1**  I am not talking about money, I am talking about our worth as a person.

**2**  Some people feel worthless:

> Too small,
> Few brains,
> Not good at sport,
> Not most important in family.

**3** The fact is we all have some talent.

> We need to identify it.

**4** If we think we are worthless, look at handicapped:

> Legless,
> Armless,
> Blind,
> Deaf and dumb.

**5** Some handicapped are born like it.

It can be worse for those to whom it happens through accident or war.

**6** Look at the Marathons (London? New York? etc.,). The handicapped take part showing courage, nerve, skill.

**7** The Paraplegic Games are held each summer at Stoke Mandeville.

It is incredible how many sports they can manage to do.

**8** Some people may regard colour as a disadvantage too.

Certainly many black people feel they are treated as handicapped.

**9** White people tempted to say they are not like us. Treat them as second-class citizens.

**10** We need to work together (all colours and creeds) towards a common goal.

**11** The story of Dr Aggrey, a Ghanaian, is helpful.

People thought because he was black he was worthless.

Became Vice Principal of a college in his country.

**12** He thought hard about colour. Then said:

'God knew what he was doing when he made me black. He did not want me to be grey or white. He wanted me to be black. On a piano you must use the black and white keys together. God wants to play tunes with his black and white notes together.'

**13** Dr Aggrey has the answer.

So called disadvantage can be turned to advantage. Can be seen positively.

**14** It is true of colour, race and handicap.

**15** Nobody can believe that it is better to have no arms or legs or be paralysed. Nor can one really believe God intended it.

**16** But handicap or racial disadvantage can bring out the best in people – courage, determination, will-power, and often a delightful personality.

**17** Think of all your blessings and you will see your true worth.

**PRAYER**

We are conscious of the many blessings that we have and of how much better off we are than many others. May those who are seriously handicapped or disadvantaged find hope and courage.

NOTES – WHAT ARE WE WORTH?

# HINDUISM – DIWALI

**1** Diwali comes from Sanskrit word:

> Deepawali = row, cluster of lights,

so it is a Festival of Lights.

**2** Celebrated by Hindus and Sikhs, usually in October or November.

(Recently Sikhs have put more emphasis on Guru Nanak's Birthday).

**3** *Hindus* celebrate it in honour of Goddess Lakshmi.

**4** Several Hindu legends associated with day:

(a) Rama, King of Ayodhya returned to his Kingdom after 14 years exile. His wife, who had been stolen by the demon King Ravana, was released and Ravana and his wicked brother were defeated.

The victory and return were celebrated with lights all over the capital.

(b) The Festival is traced back to the coronation of King Vikramaditya.

On his coronation the Hindu calendar began (48 years older than Christian).

King Vikramaditya, like King Solomon had reputation for justice.

(c) Origin of Diwali also attributed to destruction by Vishnu of demon named Naraka, sometimes called demon of dirt. Naraka they said, brought the Monsoons.

At Diwali, after heat and dust of summer and monsoon, it is time to clean houses and paint ready for illuminations.

5   In W. India Diwali marks the beginning of the New Year. Lakshmi the Goddess of Wealth is worshipped on that day and merchants open new account books.

6   The Sikhs celebrate Diwali in honour of sixth Guru, Guru Hargobind.

Guru's father was assassinated by the Mughals for refusing to change faith in 1606.

Guru refused to pay fine imposed on father for preaching so Mughal Emperor imprisoned him at Fort Gwalior. There for 5 years.

Eventually Emperor Jehangir examined Guru's case and ordered release.

Sharing prison were 52 Hindu princes. Guru said he would only accept release if princes could leave with him. Prison officers said that as many as could get through narrow passage of prison holding Guru's clothes could go free.

Guru ordered cloak to be made with long tassels at end. All princes walked to freedom holding his train.

When Guru returned to Amristar in 1620, Sikhs illuminated Golden Temple in his honour.

7   So for both Hindus and Sikhs Diwali is a time of rejoicing with lights, fireworks, exchange of sweets and a gala atmosphere.

An open lamp of burnt clay filled with ghee (rarified butter) burns throughout night at place of worship.

### A HINDU PRAYER

May all be happy. May all be free from suffering. May all see what is good. May the good attain peace. May the peaceful be free from bondage. May the free make others free.

NOTES – HINDUISM - DIWALI

# HINDUISM – DUSSEHRA

1    Hinduism so old nobody knows when it began.

2    Traceable in history to 4,000 years ago.

Aryans (nobles) from N. West invaded India.

3    Indians = people beyond river Indus.

Indus called Hindus by foreigners, hence Hindus (first the people not the religion).

4    Aryans spread religion. Large number of hymns, chants, prayers. Later written down as Vedas.

5    Gods – Brahma – Creator God
            Vishnu  – Preserver
            Siva     – Destroyer.

6    Vishnu is said to have come to earth many times, once as Lord Krishna who wrote:

'whichever God you pray to it is I who answer.'

7    Other Hindu Gods – Varuna – Sky God; Agni – Fire God

8    The priests – called Brahmins – added new writings to the Vedas called Brahamas.

These were rules for ceremonies.

9    2000–3000 years ago important writings called Upanishads were also added as commentaries to the Vedas. Upanishad means literally 'sit down near' – inviting people to come and listen to the great teachers.

10    Hindu beliefs:

(a) Re-incarnation (come back worse or better).
(b) Nirvana (state of bliss attained by ways of salvation).
(c) Ways to salvation:

        Karma – through works
        Yoga – through strict control of mind and body
        Devotion – simplest way

11    Many Hindu Festivals:

(Said in India: 13 Festivals in 12 months).

12    Dussehra is one of most popular festivals in India.

13    Celebrated for 10 days in month of Asvina (September–October).

It comprises worship of Goddess Durga –
Durga Puja (Puja = worship).
Devi, the Divine Mother, is all things to all people.

14 Images are installed in houses and public places. There is Katha ( = Storytelling) and religious music.

A Pandit, well versed in ancient lore, reads passages extolling deity and comments on them with tales and anecdotes.

15 The first nights are a period of fasting. Legend says, malicious demons who ruled the Punjab, forbade people to eat and consumed all food.

On eighth day, Goddess Durga appeared in war-like form and put demons to flight.

She asked people to feast themselves.

16 On Vijaya-Dasami (last day of Dussehra), worship of Gods, especially Lord Rama, is carried out with fervour and prayers are offered in every home.

**HINDU PRAYER**

O God, we salute the great thought of oneness which proclaims the unity of all existence, seeks the happiness and welfare of all beings and is free from all strife and conflict.

```
NOTES – HINDUISM - DUSSEHRA




```

# ISLAM – RAMADHAN

1 Ramadhan is ninth month of Muslim calendar.

(Islam follows Lunar calendar so year a little shorter 12 × 28 days and therefore date of Ramadhan varies each year).

**2** Ramadhan is month of fasting (one of 5 pillars of Islam).

Fast is feast with 'E' for eating omitted.

**3** Fasting is from dawn to dusk, compulsory for all healthy adult Muslims (exceptions: sick, pregnant, traveller, very old or infirm. For some, days missed are made up later).

**4** Reward for fasting is recorded and given by God himself.

**5** During month the Holy Book, The Quran, is read often as believed that it was revealed around 27th Ramadhan.

**6** At end of fast, great festival of Eid-Ul-Fitr. Great excitement when moon is sighted. Next day Muslims rise early and have bath. Special breakfast, including sweet dish 'Sheer Kurma' – vermicelli cooked in milk with dried dates, raisins, almonds and other nuts.

**7** All go to Mosque (separate enclosure for women) where Imam (Priest) calls out: 'Allah-o-Akbar' (Allah is the greatest). Sermon follows.

**8** Spirit of Eid is one of peace, forgiveness and brotherhood.

**9** It is family day, with great rejoicing and exotic meals. Gifts and greetings are exchanged.

In Muslim countries great fairs, folk-dancing and music.

**10** Islam = Submission and obedience to God.

Person who has submitted is Muslim.

**11** Beliefs: One God – Allah
His Angels
His Prophets
Day of Judgement
Good and Evil
Life after Death

**12** Religion built on five pillars:

(a) Shahada – No God but Allah
(b) Salat    – Prayer 5 times a day
(c) Zakat    – Giving of alms to needy
(d) Saum    – Fasting during Ramadhan
(e) Hajj     – Pilgrimage to Mecca.

**13** Mohammed – last and chief of Prophets – born about 571 AD, perfect man to whom Allah revealed The Quran.

His birth celebrated on 12th of month Rabi-ul-Awwal. Day restricted as Mohammed also died on same date.

**14** Preached in Mecca. Invited hearers to join him. Made many enemies who plotted his murder.

**15** With help of others, escaped to Medina on 20th September 622.

### MUSLIM PRAYER

From Quran

Almighty, it is thee whom we serve and on thee we call for help. Guide us in the straight way, the way of those to whom thou hast been gracious!

---

NOTES – ISLAM RAMADHAN

---

# ISLAM – HAJJ

**1** Hajj (August–September) = Pilgrimage.

One of Five Pillars of Islam.

**2** At this time Pilgrims from all over world go to Mecca in Arabia.

A Muslim makes every effort to make pilgrimage at least once in lifetime.

**3** Important rituals:

(a) Putting on Ihram.
Male Pilgrim has to replace clothes with two white sheets of seamless cloth.
Females dress in simple clothes but do not have to cover face.
(b) Making seven circuits of Kaabah, = large rectangular stone shrine;
first house ever built for worship of God; Used by Adam, Eve, Ibrahim, Ismael and Mohammed. All stand shoulder to shoulder, rich and poor, master and servant.

(c) Performing **Sa'ee.**
   Going seven times between mountains nearby, Safa and Marwan, in memory of Hagar, wife of Ibrahim who searched for water for son Ismael.
   Pilgrim drinks from sacred well of Zam-Zam.

(d) Visiting Mina, Arafat and Muzdalifah.
   (Mount Arafat was where God forgave Adam and Eve).
   Staying at Arafat is most important ritual of all. Pardon is sought for all sins and then Pilgrim becomes sinless.

4   At end of Hajj comes Eid-Ul-Adha – Festival of Sacrifice.

To commemorate God's test of Ibrahim when asked to sacrifice son Ismael.

(Jews believe Abraham was asked to sacrifice Isaac).

5   It is Festival of Thanksgiving for those who have made pilgrimage to Mecca.

6   Normally sheep, cow, etc. sacrificed for each household.

If poor, can be between 7 households.

7   Animals slaughtered. Meat divided.

Family keeps a third, rest given uncooked to poor to make a sacrifice.

8   Reminds Muslims and all religious people should be prepared to give up all for God.

**PRAYER**

May we learn from what Mohammed taught: that God accepts our sacrifice of praise and worship, together with the dedication of our lives.

---

NOTES – ISLAM HAJJ

# BUDDHISM

1    Buddhism founded by Gautama, the Buddha. Lived about 2500 years ago.

2    Born Siddhartha Gautama, son of a ruler in N. India. Was surrounded by riches and luxury.

3    Nearly thirty years old. Saw suffering and misery in world outside.

4    Sought the answers to suffering from Hindu teachers but found none.

5    He fasted but made himself ill. Then one day sat under a tree and he was 'enlightened.' Tree afterwards was called the 'Bo-Tree' – (Tree of Enlightenment).

6    This is when he became the Buddah – the Enlightened One.

7    His first sermon was given to five others who thought like him. It gave his basic belief in the middle way.

8    He preached a middle path between greed and fasting. This path gives vision, wisdom, peace and enlightenment.

9    The Buddhist Festival, Asala Puja, remembers the teaching of the middle way.

10    The Buddha taught his beliefs until his death in his eighties when he passed into Nirvana.

11    Nirvana is Leaving World, not being re-incarnated but continuing to exist.

(Gautama believed in Hindu re-incarnation by which one returns to this life many times in better or worse status according to one's life).

12    The Buddha taught the Four Noble Truths and the Eight-fold Path.

(a) *Four Noble Truths*
Suffering is part of Life
Suffering is caused by desire
Suffering will end when desire ends
The Eight-fold Path destroys suffering.

(b) *Eight-fold Path*
Right understanding, right thought, right speech, right action, right vocation, right effort, right mindfulness, right concentration.

13    Main Buddhist sacred writings are:

Tri-Pitaka (Three Baskets)
(based on image of baskets filled with earth passed one to other when building)
First basket    – Rules for Monks (Orange robes)
Second basket – Teaching basket (stories and teachings of Buddha).
Third basket    – Explanations of teachings.

**14** Buddhism gradually died out in India.

Two types of Buddhism:

> The Great Vehicle – Sri Lanka, Burma
> The Little Vehicle- Tibet, China, Korea, Japan.

**15** In Japan took name of Zen Buddhists. Discarded writings, believe in meditation.

**16** In England, Wesak is the main Buddhist Festival. Day to remember Gautama who was Founder of Buddhism.

**PRAYER**

May we understand the various values of each religion. From Buddhism let us learn unselfishness, meditation, relaxation and peace of mind.

---

NOTES – BUDDHISM

---

# HALLOWE'EN

**1** Time of Hallowe'en again – October 31st.

Called Hallowe'en because All Hallows Eve – day before All Saints Day (All Hallows).

**2** On All Saints Day – November 1st – special Christians called Saints are remembered.

**3** On All Souls Day – November 2nd – all other dead people are remembered.

**4** No ghosts, witches, wizards, warlocks, evil spirits would dare appear on All Saints Day, so they "come out to play" on Hallowe'en.

**5** Long ago, October 31st was end of Celtic year. (Pagan festival of Samain – Summer's End).

**6** Big fires lit. Lanterns made from hollowed out turnips or mangel–wurzels. (These are called Punkies in Somerset Village of Hinton St. George which celebrates Hallowe'en as Punkie Night).

**7** The fires and 'Punkies' (with horrible faces carved on them) were intended to frighten away evil spirits.

**8** Today Hallowe'en is rather a time of fun than fear. Few people now believe in evil spirits. If they do, they do not necessarily believe they come out at Hallowe'en.

**9** Nowadays it is a time for parties with people dressing up as witches, vampires, wizards or skeletons.

**10** Chestnuts are still roasted and apples baked, representing old custom of eating nuts to make them wise and apples to protect them from evil.

Young women peeled an apple in one piece and dropped the peel on the ground in hope it would form initial letter of man they would marry.

**11** Hallowe'en especially popular with children, particularly in United States.

**12** Favourite children's game in United States and now arrived in this country is "Trick or Treat."

Children in Hallowe'en costumes knock on door. If a treat (sweet buiscuit or small gift) is not given, children play a trick e.g. soaping the windows.

**13** Hallowe'en is really a time for Christians to Hallow themselves – make themselves Holy – in readiness for All Saints Day.

**14** Saints – people canonised by the Church – are those who by self-sacrifice and commitment to God have served their fellow human beings or have had a special insight into spiritual matters.

**15** On All Souls Day we think about all those – particularly family and friends – who have departed this life.

**PRAYER**

We are glad that belief in God removes all fear of evil spirits.

We remember with gratitude the lives of those of our family and friends who have now departed this life.

---

NOTES – HALLOWE'EN

# SAYING SORRY

1  Parable of Prodigal Son. (Parable is a story with a message).

   St Luke, Chapter 15, verses 11–32.

2  Jesus told story to show God forgives all who are sorry for things they have done and are prepared to admit they are wrong.

3  Not as easy as it sounds. We usually believe we are right.

4  Saying sorry is seen by many as weak, giving in.

   We often prefer to say:

   'Why should I?'

5  Charles Kingsley wrote book called 'The Water Babies.' In it a character called: Mrs Do-As-You-Would-Be-Done-By.

6  Perhaps that gives us the secret of life.

   People treat us very often in same way as we treat them.

7  If we want people to be kind, pleasant, understanding, friendly, then what about starting it first?

8  Let us think about Jesus's story.

   In one sense younger son deserved all he got.

   Selfish, greedy, thoughtless, out for a good time at everybody else's expense.

9  But he suffered for it.

   Had to keep Pigs (Pigs considered unholy and forbidden to Jews) and was so hungry, almost ate Pigs' food.

10  Then he came to his senses. Returned home and asked his Father's forgiveness.

11  So often have two standards:

   One for ourselves
   One for others.

12  'Why doesn't he/she accept my apology?' 'I've said sorry.'

   Would you say sorry?

13  Why don't people say sorry?

   Because it means saying: 'I was wrong,' and you have to swallow pride.

14  Takes great courage and people do not always accept apology.

   (Elder Brother in story).

**15** However, saying sorry often brings a resolution to the problem.

It disarms. It takes sting out of situation.

**16** In end, people are glad to accept apology and to resume normal relations.

If not, at least one feels at peace with oneself and with God.

**PRAYER**

Make us aware of our own faults and our need to ask for forgiveness. Make us slow to offend and quick to apologise so that we may all live in peace and harmony.

NOTES – SAYING SORRY

# REMEMBRANCE SUNDAY

**1** This last/coming Sunday was/is Remembrance Sunday.

**2** We remember the dead of many wars:

> 1st and 2nd World Wars
> Korea
> The Falklands
> Northern Ireland.

**3** Many millions have died.

Take the 2nd World War:

> 20 million died in battle,
> 20 million civilians were killed,
> 30 million soldiers were wounded,
> 30 million homes were destroyed,
> 150 million people were made homeless.

**4**  Who can justify that?

It is death and destruction on a horrendous scale.

**5**  War is evil but it is a moral dilemma. Can we allow an evil regime to prosper?

In the last war could we ignore the murder of millions of Jews?

**6**  We are all bound up together as Human Beings. If another nation is attacked and overrun, don't they have a right to expect others to help them?

**7**  Yet CND is a wonderful thing.

Jesus said: 'Love your enemies.'

Mahatma Gandhi said: 'No violence.'

Martin Luther King said: 'No retaliation.'

**8**  How can we bring nations to their senses?

More importantly can we bring leaders to their senses?

**9**  If only we could find another way.

Churchill once said: 'I prefer Jaw Jaw to War War.'

**10**  Can't we talk to one another and sort things out?

**11**  It is not as easy at that. It is all a question of national pride. Rights over land and money also play a big part.

**12**  Remembrance Sunday so often seems a glorification of War.

It should not be that.

**13**  It is a sad reminder of tragic events and people remember the loss of husbands, fathers, brothers, sisters, daughters, wives etc.

**14**  We have to say:

Let us remember their sacrifice.

Let us build a world of peace and friendship in their honour.

**15**  We must make the world a better place for their sake and pray that war will be no more.

**PRAYER**

Let us stand in silence for a minute.

We remember with gratitude all those who have given their lives to make this world a better place to live in. We pray for those who still suffer as a result of the war and ask that nations may learn to live together in peace, sharing the good things they have.

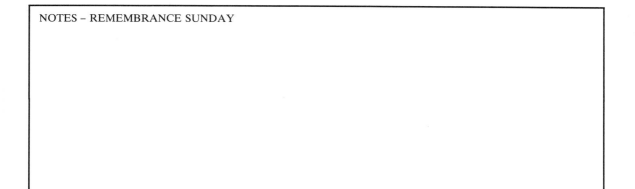

# LEAVERS ASSEMBLY

**1** Read: 1 Corinthians, Chapter 13 (from a modern version, preferably).

**2** With all our learning we do not know very much.

**3** At different stages in life different things seem important:

> Life changes
> Society changes
> *We* change.

**4** 'When I was a girl/boy . . .' quote examples.

**5** Human life is like that.

> Things come and go: People
> Events
> Places
> Jobs
> Interests.

**6** We may meet our School Friends again – probably not.

**7** But some things last for ever.

> I will mention three: *Trust
> Hope
> Love.

*These words will vary with the translation used eg Faith, Hope, Charity.

**8** *Trust*

Think of that word. Without it life is unthinkable.

 (i) The first thing employers ask is "he/she trustworthy?"
(ii) But 'Trust' has other meanings:

Taking things on Trust
Trusting others
Trusting *in* others – as some people trust in God
Trusting oneself.

**9** *Hope*

Sometimes life seems so hopeless:

"Hope springs eternal in the breast."

Does it?

(i) Without hope what would **human beings have achieved?**
(ii) In the most impossible circumstances, people do not give up.
How often we hear the words: "I never give up hope," or hope is what kept us alive."
We summon up unknown reserves.
(iii) Hope in the future. We are built to hope, to press forward.

**10** *Love*

The greatest of all is Love.

John Lennon's song: Love is the answer.
The Pope　　　　　: Love is greater than hate.

(i) Not just romantic love – although that is included.
(ii) If love were present everywhere there would be:

No selfishness
No unkindness
No rudeness
No unfairness
No prejudice
No snobbishness
No boasting
No hatred.

**11** The passage we read says:

Love is tough – it can face everything.

**12** These three things: Trust, Hope and Love are the greatest because they come from God.

They are divine qualities.

**PRAYER**

A prayer of St. Francis of Assisi:

Eternal God, the Father of all mankind: we commit to thee the needs of the whole world: where there is hatred, give love; where there is injury, pardon; where there is distrust, faith; where there is sorrow, hope; where there is darkness, light (*through Jesus Christ our Lord). *Optional in multi-faith assemblies.

NOTES – LEAVERS ASSEMBLY

GENERAL NOTES

# 6th Form Assemblies

# POWER OF SPEECH

1   This morning/afternoon, I want to speak to you about ....................................

2   The power of speech. One of our faculties (powers)

>   Speaking
>   Hearing
>   Seeing
>   Feeling
>   Smelling.

3   When human life, as we understand it, began humans (being animals) made animal noises.

4   Basic sounds – grunt, moan, squeal, shout, cry, laugh.

5   When life was basic, that was all that was needed. Most animals still at that stage.

6   What does a dog's bark mean? and does "two barks" mean something else?

7   Birds sing songs – or do they?

    It seems clear that birds use their "songs" to call young when in danger, or to woo their mate or signal there is food about.

8   Bats emit a radar that warns them of obstacles they might hit.

9   Apes, in U.S.A. experiments, are being taught primitive speech.

    Some of us enjoy animals 'acting' in advertisements.

10  But so far, humans are the only ones to develop speech with complex language that does not just express feelings.

11  Human beings can be deeply thought-provoking and intellectual.

12  Humans need to use sophisticated, complex language to express technical and abstract ideas.

13  No other animal has been able to express thoughts about the universe and debate the existence of a God.

14  Humans are the only animals which are both actors and spectators.

    We may be tiny but we express our thoughts about everything in Life, big or small.

15  Speech gave birth to writing and recording. Writing is what puts humans in an impregnable position in the world.

16 As far as we know, no other animal can record its thoughts.

They are born with natural instincts and actions but nothing to learn from the previous generations.

17 A tape, a video, a record, a book preserves for posterity human thinking and achievement.

18 We do not have to start from scratch. There is a wealth of knowledge and experience in store.

19 It is speech and writing that make humans unique, the all powerful dominating animal.

20 Is this what is meant by God breathed into Man's nostrils the breath of life and he became a living soul?

```
NOTES – POWER OF SPEECH



```

# POLLUTION

THEME: God has made this world beautiful but man has spoilt it.

(This can be used as a debate in Assembly).

1 You may question this:

e.g. Earthquakes, Hurricanes, Tornadoes, Snow, Ice, Volcanoes etc.

2 We may accuse God but it is man who has ruined the earth.

e.g. biggest epidemic of our time is death on the roads.

3 The earth is about 4,500 million years old. Humans have been around for about 50,000 years (1/800th of time).

4 Farming was properly started about 10,000 years ago.

5 Then Humans began to alter their surroundings:

e.g. development of: use of metals, writing
    beginninng of: science
    growth of: towns and cities.

6  250 years ago: start of industrialisation and acceleration of population growth.

7  Today Humans have the means, the technology to interfere with Life on Planet.

8  Life on our planet exists in the Biosphere – the thin layer which is the meeting place of land, air and water.

    Downwards in earth or sea          6 miles
    Upwards in mountains               6 miles

9  70% of Earth's surface is uninhabitable for humans in comfort:

    sea, swamps, mountains, ice, deserts etc.

10  After that very little is left.

    So what are we doing with it?

    (a) Water pollution – poisonous wastes; one third of English lakes are dead.
    (b) Oil is fouling beaches and killing sea birds.
    (c) Electricity uses water and this water is discharged warm into rivers killing fish and eggs.
    (d) Smoke in the air, petrol fumes, lead in petrol.
        90–100 people a day in Britain die from Bronchitis.
    (e) Exhausts from jets stopping the sunlight reaching the Earth, making it colder.
    (f) Poisonous fall-out from nuclear tests and disasters.
    (g) Dumping of nuclear waste in the seas.
    (h) Dangerous chemicals (e.g. DDT) get into drinking water and into bodies of humans and other animals.
    (i) Noise pollution – deafness from excessive decibels.
        The level at which noise interferes with sleep is 50–55 decibels. The noise from a car makes 70 decibels.

11  There is a hymn which begins:

    Turn back, O Man, forswear thy foolish ways.

NOTES – POLLUTION

# EVIL AND SUFFERING

1   Often evil and suffering are closely connected.

2   (Think of some of the evil things that people think, say and write).

3   Thinking may sound harmless but evil is often planned.

  People work out how they are going to hurt, maim, kill somebody or bodies.

4   People Murder
      Rape
      Abuse children
      Burgle houses
      Rob old people
      Mug passersby and so on.

5   Sometimes one wonders whether the whole world has become sick and twisted.

6   We must never forget that what we do affects other people – for good or bad.

7   What are your principles?

  Our aim must be to do the greatest good to the greatest number of people.

8   But, of course, suffering is not always caused by evil people.

9   A great deal is caused by natural disasters:

      Earthquakes
      Hurricanes
      Tornadoes
      Drought
      Floods
      Tidal Waves
      Cyclones
      Volcanoes, and so on.

10   The question may well be asked:

      How can a good God allow such terrible things to happen? (If there is a God?).

11   There is no simple answer.

  It certainly does not appear to be punishment – although some religions believe this.

12   But how could (name a recent disaster) be a punishment?

13   No, the truth is it has not really anything to do with God.

**14** We know why there are earthquakes, volcanoes, droughts etc.

They come from the interplay of fixed laws.

**15** To avoid a disaster God would have to intervene and suspend the natural laws for a while.

**16** And where would we be then?

**17** We only survive because we can depend absolutely on Nature's Laws.

**18** Gravitation. What would happen to us all if momentarily it were suspended?

**19** What if you tried to boil a kettle and instead it froze?

**20** But if Laws are fixed – and we need them fixed – then sometimes people will suffer.

**21** Just to finish:

(i) Without suffering, pain, problems, difficulties, Humankind would never have advanced. It is by overcoming problems that we have reached this stage of civilisation.

(ii) Without suffering, etc., there would be no need for sympathy and loving care.

NOTES – EVIL AND SUFFERING

# BELIEF IN GOD

**1** Years ago startling headline appeared in newspaper:

"GOD IS DEAD"

**2** What did it mean?

Not that God had suddenly died of old age.

**3** It meant the idea of God existing had died.

> Humans had grown up.
> God was only for primitive savages – not for educated, scientific, humans of 20th Century.

**4** It was claimed: God had only existed in the mind.

**5** Yet the vast majority of people in the world still believe in God.

**6** Many critics would say this is because of:

(a) Fear
(b) Tradition or place of birth
(c) Teaching as a child.

**7** This is in part true:

But does not really answer why religion has remained for so long.

**8** There are three classical theological arguments for belief in God:

Technical terms:

> A. Ontological
> B. Cosmological
> C. Teleological

**9** What do they mean?

A ONTOLOGICAL
Idea of God is already in human mind. Nobody puts it there, it is natural to us to believe in God. (History of all Tribes) – no record of any tribe anywhere in history without a belief in God.

B COSMOLOGICAL
All around us we see things that are the result of something else happening first.
Everything is changing. Evolution is change but what causes change? It is all cause and effect.
We trace it all back until we arrive at the first cause – God.

C TELEOLOGICAL
Everywhere we look there is pattern, logic, design.
This argument says if there is design then there must be a designer.

> (Watch – Watchmaker).

God is the Great Designer.

**10** Of course there are other arguments to show there is no God.

Very few are atheist – (do not believe in God).

Most are agnostic (are not sure).

11  The best belief in God does not come from argument but from being absolutely sure, right inside.

This is called Faith.

(At the end of this Assembly ask for a 6th Former to put arguments against God at the next Assembly).

NOTES – BELIEF IN GOD

# 1984

1  Book written by George Orwell in 1948. He simply changed the date 48 to 84.

2  He thought state he was describing with 'Big Brother' was just round the corner.

3  He was nearer the truth than he imagined.

4  In the book is the State of Oceania. Life consists of power. The Party seeks power for power's sake.

5  No room for individuals or personal relationships.

No 'I' just 'we' and that 'we' is 'Big Brother.'

6  You must not think for yourself – in fact not think at all.

7  The official language is 'Newspeak' which makes thinking impossible. It is a reduction in words and a reduction in thought.

8  The past only exists as the Party wishes it. People and events can be erased at a stroke.

9  The main character is Winston. His job is to change past newspaper reports in keeping with current views.

10     Everywhere are posters saying:

                 'Big Brother is watching you.'

11     In everybody's room there are cameras and TV screens.

12     At 11.00 a.m. every day there are two minutes of hate. Winston felt compelled to join in.

     Object of hate: Eurasia and Emmanuel Goldstein – traitor and rival to Big Brother.

13     Winston begins a relationship with Julia but this is forbidden in Oceania.

14     Winston is a rebel and believes O'Brien is a fellow conspirator but he betrays Winston and Julia.

15     Winston arrested by Thought Police.

     People arrested every day and never heard of again.

16     Winston is tortured by O'Brien himself but believes he can resist.

17     But finally he is taken to the dreaded Room 101.

18     Still thinks he can resist but everybody has a breaking point.

19     O'Brien remembers Winston hates rats.

     O'Brien says:

     'The mask will fit over your head, leaving no exit. When I press this other lever the door of the cage will slide up. These starving brutes will shoot out of it like bullets. Have you ever seen a rat leap through the air? They will leap on to your face and bore straight into it. Sometimes they attack the eyes first. Sometimes they burrow through the cheeks and devour the tongue.'

20     Winston panicked and almost lost consciousness but when he could smell the rats and saw them close to his face, he finally broke and shouted:

     'Do it to Julia: do it to Julia! Not me! Julia! I don't care what you do to her.'

21     There was nothing left for Winston. He had been beaten, broken. All that was left for him now was to love Big Brother.

22     Is this so far from the truth?

23     Look around the world. It is happening all over.

24     Now perhaps you can understand why we fight so hard for individual freedom?

25     Any threat against it, whether in this country or anywhere else must be vigorously resisted and removed.

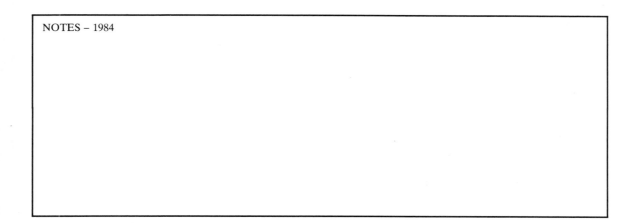

# EASTER

**1**  Imagine nearly two thousand years ago:

        Jerusalem
        First Easter Sunday.

**2**  Little group of men and women are meeting to decide what to do.

    Jesus, their leader, is dead, and his body sealed in a tomb.

**3**  The previous Friday as the Disciples watched Jesus on the Cross they believed he would save himself miraculously.

**4**  The crowd shouted: 'If you are the Son of God, come down from the Cross.'

**5**  There is even a tradition that Judas Iscariot only betrayed him because he believed Jesus would perform a miracle and come down from the Cross thus publicly proclaiming he was the Real Messiah, The Christ.

**6**  With the Sabbath (Saturday) now over, some women decided to visit the Tomb to pay their respects.

**7**  Imagine their astonishment –

        Stone rolled away,
        No body,
        Linen clothes folded up.

**8**  Two men (Angels?) said:

    'Why do you look for the Living among the Dead?'

**9**  Did Jesus rise from the dead?

    Many question it.

**10** A famous book 'Passover Plot' by Hugh Schonfield, puts forward an alternative explanation.

**11** He claims Jesus planned it all but had no intention of dying.

He was given drugged wine and the drug used gave all the appearances of death, so suggested Mr Schonfield.

**12** What, he added, Jesus had not bargained for was the soldier thrusting his spear into his side.

**13** Schonfield continues with the view that Jesus recovered from the drug on the Sunday (remember Jews were not buried but placed in a cave) but because of his mortal wound died 40 days later. (When the Bible claims he ascended to Heaven).

**14** The Christian claims that nobody at the time suggested that the resurrection was a trick, and Pilate went to great lengths (a Guard and a Seal) to ensure there was no trickery.

**15** We do know that a frightened demoralised band of Disciples suddenly changed to a vibrant assured group of convinced believers who founded the Christian Church.

**16** Should we believe it? It is a question of religious faith.

**17** It is no different from belief in Guru Gobind Singh or the stories of Mohammed or Gautama Buddha.

**18** Each religion believes and treasures its own set of:

Sacred books
Sacred leaders
Sacred stories.

**19** So with Easter: on Easter Sunday the Christian shouts:

'Christ is risen! Hallelujah!'

NOTES – EASTER

# CAUSE AND EFFECT

1   If you could have anything you wanted, what would you ask for?

        Win pools?
        Pass exams?
        Fall in love?
        Get a good job?

2   It may be corny but it is often said that the best things in life are free.

3   How high on your list would *health* be?

4   There is a great deal of suffering in the world.

5   As one disease is cured another appears.

    We conquer T.B. then Cancer takes over.

6   And now the dreaded killer disease is AIDS and nobody yet can find a cure.

7   Sometimes we blame God.

    (a) People have even suggested God sent suffering as a punishment e.g. AIDS.
    (b) If He does not punish with disease, at least why doesn't He stop it?

8   A lot of disease is caused by Human beings themselves:

    e.g. Lack of hygiene
         Lack of precautions (boiling water)
         Unhealthy practices.

9   Suffering is also caused by humans who deliberately injure or kill others:

    e.g. Drunken drivers
         Terrorists
         War
         Deliberate contamination of food.

10   Suffering is also caused by natural disasters.

    Here again people argue that a good God would stop natural disasters.

11   If the natural laws were suspended to avoid a disaster, chaos would ensue.

12   The only way we can survive is because we can be 100% sure that natural laws are fixed.

13   It might be wonderful if someone could be saved from throwing themselves out of a 15th floor window by suspending gravitation.

    The rest of the world would then fly into space.

14    What if we went to boil a kettle and it froze instead?

15    Laws are essential.

16    God is not all-powerful in this context. The laws he has made govern everything.

17    God has also given us free-will. This means we can freely choose.

It is the one thing that makes us human and makes life worth living.

18    The consequence of free-will is that we can choose good or evil.

We can choose to harm or kill someone.

19    It is sad that so often it is the good and the innocent who suffer most.

20    This cannot be avoided as we are all bound up with one another, the good with the bad.

21    The one lesson we all have to learn is that everything we do affects other people for good or evil. Never let us imagine that it is just up to us how we behave.

---

NOTES – CAUSE AND EFFECT

---

# FUTURE SHOCK

1    Title of book by Alvin Toffler.

2    It means: The Disease of Change.

3    Change is process by which future invades our lives.

4    Toffler (wrote in 1970s) –

"In 3 decades between now and 21st Century millions of ordinary people will face an abrupt collision with future."

**5** Some say: this is second Industrial Revolution.

Toffler: It's second great divide in history.
(First: barbarism – civilisation).

**6** This divide actually running through our lifetime.

**7** He says: take last 500,000 years of human existence.

Divide into lifetimes of 62 years = 800 Lifetimes.

   (i) 650 of those spent in caves
  (ii) Last 6: Masses used printed word.
 (iii) Last 4: Precise measurement of time.
 (iv) Last 2: Electric motor.
  (v) This lifetime: majority of all material goods we use.

**8** Most significant thing is pace of change. Characteristic of present life-span is impermanence and transience.

**9** In March 1967 in Eastern Canada an 11 year-old boy died of old age.

Had lived a biologically complete life – senility, baldness, wrinkles, hardened arteries.

**10** Not all becoming senile but experiencing super-human rates of change.

**11** Take transportation:

| | | |
|---|---|---:|
| 6000 BC–camel | – | 8 mph |
| 1825 –steam loco | – | 100 mph |
| 1938 –airplane | – | 400 mph |
| 1960s –rocket | – | 4,800 mph |
| –men in space | – | 18,000 mph |

**12** Draw a graph and you get a shock.

**13** And now we have computers, lasers etc.

**14** Our ancestors could expect to live their lives very much as their fathers did.

**15** But now it is 'The Vanishing Past.'

(a) Houses knocked down.
(b) New one-way systems.
(c) Countryside disappearing.

**16** We live in 'throw-away society.'

     Trade-in cars
     Paper clothes.

**17** Tragically there is also an impermanence of relationships.

**18**   To sum up: we are bombarded by change. More has happened in this lifespan than in the whole of previous history.

**19**   We have got to learn to cope, survive and conquer.

**20**   Some suggested strategies:

        (a) Relaxation and organisation.
        (b) Taming of technology.
        (c) Education in future tense, (anticipation of direction of change).
        (d) Social futurism.
          (i) Time horizons must be extended.
         (ii) More advanced democratic feedback.
       (iii) Whole society to be made part of decision-making process.

---

NOTES – FUTURE SHOCK

---

# TO HAVE OR TO BE

**1**   Dr. Erich Fromm, the philosopher, died in 1980, born in Germany, left for U.S.A. in 1934.

Books: *Art of Loving, Escape from Freedom, Man For Himself.*

In 1976 wrote: '*To Have Or To Be.*'

A new blueprint for mankind.

**2**   To have is a normal function.

To live we must have things.

**3**   That is the supreme goal of our culture.

e.g. being worth a million dollars.

If one *has* nothing, one *is* nothing.

**4**   Verb 'to have' is becoming more common.

        I have a problem.
        I have insomnia.
        I have a beautiful wife.

106

**5** However, a few years ago one would have said:

> I am troubled.
> I cannot sleep.
> I am happily married.

**7** People even say: 'I have a great love for you.'

This is a contradiction in words.

Love is emptying. Total giving.

**8** This 'having' is gradually consuming us all.

There has been a great promise of unlimited progress.

> Domination of nature.
> Material abundance
> Greatest happiness for greatest number.

**9** Industrial age made us think we were really on way:

> Unlimited production
> Unlimited consumption.

**10** Now we realise limits.

> Not only personally
> But nationally and globally.

**11** Humans are destroying the world (Ecology).
Destroying themselves.

**12** A change of heart is needed.

> Fromm quotes:

> *Buddha*: To arrive at highest state of Human development, we must not crave possessions.

> *Jesus*: What shall it profit a man if he gain the whole world and lose his own soul?

> *Marx*: Luxury is as much a vice as poverty.

> *Master Eckhart*: (13th century Dominican Teacher)
> The person who wants nothing is the person who is not greedy for anything.

**13** To sum up. From uses two contrasting poems:
(i) *Tennyson*
  "Flower in a crannied wall
  I pluck you out of the crannies
  I hold you here, root and all, in my hand."
  ('Pluck' – 'Root and all' – Must *have* it – Western attitude).

(ii) *Basho* (17th Century Japanese poet)
"When I look carefully
I see the Nazuna blooming
by the hedge."
(Wants only to see it, and to be at one with it).

14 Difference between being and having is not essentially difference between East and West.

15 Rather between a society centred round persons or centred round things.

---

NOTES – TO HAVE OR TO BE

---

# THE AESTHETIC

1 I want to quote a famous poem called 'Leisure' written by William Davies, who died in 1940:

'What is this life if full of care
We have no time to stand and stare
No time to stand beneath the boughs
and stare as long as sheep and cows.'

2 It goes on to say that it is a poor life if we do not have time to enjoy the beauties of nature.

3 You may not feel you have much time.

Especially if you are taking 'A' Levels.

4 But what about after June?

5 Trouble with life: it has become a rat race.

6 Progress is, for most people, to go faster and faster. Quality of life not considered.

7   People are concerned with end-product.

    What use is it?

8   So in schools:

> Practical
> Technical
> Vocational.

9   Why bother with Art, Drama, Music?

    They will not necessarily get you a job.

10   But they can give you an exciting, creative and satisfying life.

11   If we divided up the timetable according to relevance to future life we would have to give the largest slice to music. We are listening to music almost all the time.

12   We need time to stand and stare.

    To wonder.

13   And so poetry: writing it, appreciating it.

14   The Queen/King has a chosen poet:

> The Poet Laureate (Give name).

15   On St George's Day each year we also remember the birthday of William Shakespeare (1564).

16   Here is part of a famous Sonnet of his:

> Shall I compare thee to a Summer's Day?
> Thou art more lovely and more temperate
> Rough winds do shake the darling buds of May
> And Summer's lease hath all too short a date.
> ...........But thy eternal summer shall not fade.

17   Take trouble to dip into the works of the Lake poets: Wordsworth, Coleridge, Southey.

18   Here is the beginning of a famous poem by Wordsworth:

> I wandered lonely as a cloud
> That floats on high o'er vales and hills
> When all at once I saw a crowd,
> A host, of golden Daffodils;
> Beside the lake, beneath the trees,
> Fluttering and dancing in the breeze.

19   What about an Assembly where a few of you read your favourite poem?

20   Do not forget: not only the scientific, technological, practical, mathematical and so on.

21   ALSO The Aesthetic – appreciation of the beautiful.

22   The magic of a painting, a piece of music, a poem or a daffodil.

---

NOTES – THE AESTHETIC

---

# RACISM

1   Almost every day we read about South Africa.

2   This is because of the way the Whites treat the Blacks.
    (White South Africans often have a different viewpoint).

3   Laws known as Apartheid stated:

    The Blacks:

    (a) Had to be kept apart.
    (b) Should be treated differently
    (c) Had to carry a Pass.
    (d) Were not allowed to take jobs White people were doing.

4   There have been some reforms and relaxation since Apartheid was introduced, but the divide between Black and White largely remains.

5   In 1943 an English missionary, Trevor Huddleston, went to South Africa, to Sophiatown, in Johannesburg area, where many Black people lived.

6   Most appalling slum conditions.
    Worked there for 12 years.

**7**  On 10th February 1955 Police moved into Sophiatown and everybody was forced to leave. Then their homes were destroyed.

**8**  Trevor Huddleston sat down and wrote a book about it all called:

*'Nought For Your Comfort.'*

This book shocked the world.

**9**  People now are campaigning all over the world for racial equality in South Africa.

**10**  The Organisation of African Unity (The O.A.U.), which represents most of the African states, condemns South Africa.

**11**  Yet the sad thing is that some of those countries have shown racism themselves.

**12**  Take Uganda for example.

President Amin oppressed the Asians and then threw them all out. Most came to Britain.

**13**  Black people say 'Racism is a 'White' person's problem.'

**14**  But it makes no difference what colour you are, you can still be racist:

Black v Brown
White v Black
Brown v White, and so on.

**15**  Of course, usually the majority v minority.

**16**  Why? Because 'They' want to maintain power, rights, way of life. 'They' see strangers, foreigners as a threat. 'They' do not like people who are different.

**17**  Notice I said 'They.'

But it should often be 'We.'

Because we can all be like this.

**18**  By nature, we humans are cruel, unkind, nasty:

e.g. mocking disabled e.g. 'four-eyes'
'spastic'
'boss-eyed.'

**19**  And so with colour.

**20**  The Whites have practised racism till now because they had money, guns, power.

**21**  Is there anybody here who can honestly say there is no racism in me?

**22**  Well, what are we going to do about it?

NOTES – RACISM

# AIMS OF THE SCHOOL

**1** If you went and asked a local industrialist what his aims were, what do you think he would say?

> A good product
> Satisfied customer
> Good staff relationships
> Efficient workforce.

**2** He might say all these things.

They would be true but in the end it is *profit* that counts, other things subordinate.

**3** What would you say are the School's aims?

> Good exam results?
> Control?
> Knowledge?
> Good citizens?
> Employment?
> Higher education?

**4** In a way all are right.

(Go through school aims).

**5** For example, exams. Good exam results are a priority for any school.

**6** In old grammar schools:

> Work hard, pass exams, behave well, dress well, speak well, play well.
> and
> all will be well.

**7** Sounds fine. Still partly true but now different world:

> Jobs few
> Technology high
> Communications sophisticated
> Competition cut throat
> Life constantly changing.

**8** So school has much more demanding role:

> Problem solving
> Self-confidence
> Independence
> Adaptability.

**9** In past: turned out hundreds of little models all identical. Society fitted them in to all its little slots.

**10** Now: there are no slots: or slots keep changing shape.

**11** More than exams:

> Have ideas of own
> Interview well
> Get on with other people
> Solve problems

**12** To sum up: it is the individual that counts, and it is the whole person:

> Ability
> Attitudes
> Being self-possessed.

**13** That is why you should be glad you stayed at school.

**14** Colleges may spend more time on 'A' Levels, but universities and employers prefer school product.

**15** Because they are interested not only in what you have achieved –

> but what you are.

NOTES – AIMS OF THE SCHOOL

# A MEANING TO LIFE

1   Albert Camus – French writer – born Algiers 1913 died road accident 1960.

2   Wrote '*L' Etranger*' – translated '*Outsider*'

Book available in paperback translation.

3   Main character – Meursault. Clerk in Algiers.

Young middle-class bachelor.

4   Seems to lack basic emotions and reactions.

5   Two significant events:

(a) Mother dies in an old people's home.

   (i) Meursault's employer puzzled at Meursault's lack of reaction.
   (ii) When Meursault arrives at old people's home he refuses to look at body.
   (iii) He smoked a cigarette in mother's presence.

(b) Killing of Arab.

   (i) Meursault takes gun away from his friend, Raymond, to stop him using it against Arab.
   (ii) Later Meursault comes face to face with Arab.
   (iii) Shoots Arab. Fires further four bullets into inert body.

6   Meursault put on trial for murder.

Condemned as heartless, inhuman.

Why? Because  (i) He showed indifference at Mother's death. Refused to see body. Smoked a cigarette and drank. Next day went to see comedy film.
   (ii) Shot Arab a further four times.

7   For Camus, Meursault is Mr Anybody.

Obeys doctrine of absurd. Life has no meaning. There is no past, future, code of ethics or God.

8   To exist is happiness and happiness is of the moment.

9   Enjoy now. Do not live better, live more.

10   Meursault entirely given up to sensation.

Lives only in successive moments. When sensation disappears, moment vanishes.

11   Meursault is an 'outsider' to:

(a) The reader
(b) Himself
(c) Those around him.

**12** He cannot give meaning to life.

**13** All of us need to find a meaning for our own lives.

**14** The formative years of childhood and adolescence help to make us what we are.

**15** But at 17 and 18 we often begin to examine what we believe and what we have been told.

**16** You are possibly going through that stage now. It can be very traumatic.

**17** Schools play their part in helping young people to think for themselves and establish their own values and beliefs.

**18** Can you find meaning to life?

Or, like Meursault, does it all seem absurd?

---

NOTES – A MEANING TO LIFE

---

# MARTIN LUTHER KING

**1** Martin Luther King:

Born : 15th January 1929 in Atlanta, Georgia.

Shot Dead : 4th April, 1968, Memphis, Tennessee.

**2** Probably know some of story, and some of famous speeches he made.

**3** For example he said:

'19,000,000 Blacks are second class citizens,'

and

'Sunday is most segregated day of week.'

**4** Significant event in struggle of Blacks for equality. The 'Bus Boycott' in 1955, Alabama.

**5** On buses: invisible dividing line:

> Black at back
> White at front

*But* Blacks could sit in middle *only*

> if no *Whites* wanted a seat
> if *one* White needed a seat, the whole row of Blacks had to leave.

**6** 1955: Mrs Rosa Parks, Black, boarded bus, sat in middle, refused to move. Said she was too tired.

**7** 'O.K. Nigger,' said Driver 'I'll have you arrested.' Fined $10.

**8** Blacks boycotted buses for 381 days.

Brought bus company to its knees.

**9** What are facts about Blacks in U.S.A.?

One third as much chance of getting to College
One third as much chance of joining the Professions
Life expectancy 7 years less
Half as much chance of making money.

**10** In 1963 Martin Luther King made famous speech:

> 'Let Blood flow,
> *our* blood.'

> 'We shall overcome one day.'

> 'I have a dream . . .
> that my four little children one day . . .
> will not be judged by colour of skin but
> by content of their character.'

**11** What about this country?

> Are there equal opportunities?
> Do we judge people by colour of skin?
> Do we regard Blacks as second class citizens?

**12** Black and brown people have settled in communities to share their culture but also for protection, to feel safe.

**13** Often they have the worst accommodation, and the lowest jobs.

**14** What can be done?

> Is the Law the answer?

**15** How can we fulfil Martin Luther's dream?

He talked about us all being Brothers and Sisters.

**16** Martin Luther King believed in non-violence but met a violent death.

**17** In the end it is people's attitudes that have to be overcome –

Pride, Intolerance, Prejudice.

---

NOTES – MARTIN LUTHER KING

---

# UNIQUENESS OF "MAN?"

**1** The writer of one of the Psalms in Old Testament, speaking to God said:

'When I consider thy heavens, the work of thy fingers,
The moon and stars which thou hast ordained
What is man, that thou art mindful of him?'

**2** What is man? How small and insignificant human beings are! Especially when you look at the sky.

**3** Sunrise, sunset, light, darkness, moon, stars on a starlit night.

**4** There are 100,000 million stars, each one like sun on its own.

**5** Many stars much more powerful than sun.

**6** Even the Sun is 93,000,000 miles away and light from it takes 8 minutes to reach us.

**7** Distance of Sun and Stars is measured in Light Years.

Light travels 186,000 miles per second, so a Light Year =

$186,000 \times 60(\text{secs}) \times 60(\text{mins}) \times 24(\text{hrs}) \times 365(\text{days}) = $ approximately 6 million million miles.

**8**    The nearest Star is 4.50 light years away.

Thus $4.50 \times 6$ million million $= 27$ million, million miles away.

**9**    When we look at the sky we are not actually seeing what is there.

The light takes so long to travel to us that some stars we see are no longer there. Other new stars are not yet visible to us.

**10**    Look up at the Pole Star. We are seeing it as it was 680 years ago.

**11**    Light from some stars has been travelling for thousands of years.

**12**    Conversely light travelling outwards from our planet is taking thousands of years to reach the stars.

**13**    No being has yet been discovered elsewhere in the Universe but say there were? They could be watching Joan of Arc or Cromwell as the light reaches them.

**14**    This is a sobering thought: that our actions never die – they are travelling eternally through space.

**15**    When we consider all this, where does it leave insignificant 'Man?'

What is 'Man,' that thou art mindful of him?

**16**    We may be small but as far as we know we are the only creatures which are both actors and spectators in the drama of Universe.

**17**    We may be small but we can study whole Universe, discuss it, analyse it, understand it.

What other creature can do that?

**18**    This is what has led hosts of people over the history of humans to believe 'Man' is unique.

That God has given humans a soul and this soul links them to God to whom it returns on death.

---

NOTES – UNIQUENESS OF "MAN"

---

# BUILDING A JUST SOCIETY

1 Do you believe that our present society is just?

If not, how can we change it?

2 Imagine setting up a new community on a remote, uninhabited island.

3 A fresh start:

Terrible things wrong now.

Next time we can avoid them.

4 What would you do?

Four decisions to make:

        (a) Organisation
        (b) Law and Order
        (c) Marriage
        (d) Rebellion

5 Imagine community discussing these four, A, B, C, & D.

With two opposing points of view: (i) and (ii)

A Organisation.

 (i) We must all sit down and talk.
    All important decision taken by whole community.
    Everyone consulted and involved.
    Silent majority must not remain silent.
    *Only way to create new society*.
(ii) Some people are natural leaders.
    We need a leader; a small committee, obvious who they should be.
    You can have election but foregone conclusion.
    Natural leaders are more active, contribute more e.g. organise food, shelter.
    They have a right to be Leaders.
    If not they will make trouble, they are stronger.

B Law and Order

(One day H has an argument and kills one of community).

 (i) He/she is dangerous, lunatic must be got rid of.
    If no action taken, who will be next?
(ii) What sort of society developing?
    Poor pathetic H. He/she is no danger, seems harmless, frustrated, misunderstood.
    Has society driven him/her to this?

Is he/she treated properly?
It is our fault.

C Marriage and Children

(i) Proper marriages, proper ceremony.
Clear distinctions. Either people officially together or not at all.
Permission needed. If thought unsuited should be refused.

(ii) Do not make a Fuss.
If two people want to live together, let them.
It is their business, nobody else's.
If children born, put in a communal nursery.
People do not have time to bring up children.

D Rebellion

(Three young people quarrel with older member, run away and set up separate camp).

(i) We have proper channels.
Must stamp this out once and for all.
Must be captured, brought back, made to say sorry, have head shaved.
Must never happen again.

(ii) We need young life.
This is a tragedy.
Must learn from it.
Welcome them back.
Violence is wrong.
We must not use force.
*We must adapt our society*. Become too rigid.

**6** What do you think?

Does it not sound very different?
Is that because human nature does not change and societies are built on that?

**7** Society is made up of the likes of you and me.

Unless we change, society will remain the same.

**8** Would anybody here like to present a possible format for a new society?

(Next week? Another day? etc.)

---

NOTES – BUILDING A JUST SOCIETY

---

# DEATH

1   However much we try, we cannot stop time, it marches on.

2   At F.A. Cup Final, the hymn 'Abide With Me' is sung. It contains the words:

'Swift to its close ebbs out life's little day,'

and again,

'Change and decay in all around I see.'

3   Childhood, youth, maturity, old age follow closely on one another.

4   Every now and then we are reminded that we are mortal – particularly when someone well known to us dies.

It could be A schoolfriend
            A member of the family
            A national figure

5   At such moments we pause and think:

What is life all about?
Why are we here?
Where did we come from?
Where are we going to?

6   A click of the fingers – someone is there, another click of the fingers – and they are not.

7   You do not have to be old to die, it can come anytime, any place.

8   What use then the rat-race?

9   Look at people every day:

rushing to work; rushing home; worrying about success or failure, making ends meet.

10  Why bother? If death can happen any time and after a short time nobody remembers you.

11  But the strange paradox of life is:

(a) Without purpose we would die. Pushing on gives meaning to life.
(b) With zeal and purpose and hard work we kill ourselves.

12  We as humans are normally only satisfied if we have a goal to aim at.

13  Death, unfortunately, is something we hide now in the western world.

At one time people lived with it all the time. Life expectancy was very short and numbers of people died young.

14  In other parts of the world grief and mourning are much more public.

15  We need to weep and mourn and face death in its reality.

It is a fact of life and nobody has ever escaped it.

16  For most, death is not believed to be the end.

The After-Life is not just sentimental slush but a rational argument. The whole of nature teaches us that there is always resurrection and rebirth.

```
NOTES – DEATH



```

# DISHONESTY

1  Dishonesty comes in many forms. It applies to all levels of society.

2  Stealing is recognised as wrong, or is it?

3  We call it 'Fiddling,' 'Shoplifting.'
Sounds more acceptable.

4  Dishonesty is found in all walks of life:
Doctors, dockers, university lecturers, waiters.

5  More recently – computer operators, stockbrokers.

6  In fact, Dishonesty part of human life.

7  There are those who call the world of work a jungle: 'the menagerie of work.'

8  Everybody is competing and many succeed on other people's backs.

9 Is it possible, for instance, to become a millionaire without cheating somebody or making a shady deal?

10 Gerald Mars. (*author of 'Cheats at Work'*), divided the workforce in four groups;

Hawks, donkeys, wolves, vultures.

11 He was asserting that dishonesty does not exist at one level or in one group only, but in all work groups.

12 Why do you think, then, that he chose the four groups I just mentioned?

(*Wait for answer or ask them to think about it and tell you another time*).

13 Some people say:

'The bigger the firm, the greater the dishonesty.'

14 Big firms are impersonal, no sense of loyalty, no conscience.

15 In a small business, dishonesty affects your workmate or your boss you know personally.

16 Dishonesty is everywhere but not everybody is dishonest, thank God.

17 'Fiddlers' are parasites and they live off the honest.

18 If there were no 'Fiddlers'

Work would be easier
Life would be sweeter
Goods would be cheaper.

19 Every big retail company puts aside a huge sum every year to offset 'shoplifting.'

20 Are honest people 'mugs'?

No, they are the backbone of the workforce.

The foundation of society.

21 And there are many, many, more honest people than we imagine.

22 To be honest gives the individual inner satisfaction and peace.

23 More importantly, trust is generated within community.

24 School, for example. We all depend on everyone else's honesty.

25 When things go missing, we all become twitchy and nervous.

26 The Ten Commandments included one of the basic rules of society:

'Thou Shalt Not Steal.'

# THIRD WAVE

**1** Book sequel to *Future Shock* see page 104

*Re-cap*:

Strategies are needed to meet the collision with the future, to cope with tomorrow.

**2** *Questions to ask*:

Is a new civilisation being formed? Where do we fit in? Do today's technological changes and social upheavals mean the end of friendship, love, commitment, community, and caring? Will tomorrow's electronic marvels make human relationships even more vacuous and vicarious than they are today?

**3** For evidence look at the rising rates of:

> Juvenile suicide
> Alcoholism
> Depression
> Vandalism
> Crime

**4** There is a harrassed knife-edge quality to life:

> Short fuses
> 'Weirdos'
> Loneliness

**5** What must be done?

**6** Community is crumbling. So first we must attack loneliness, examples of which are:

> Strangers in launderettes
> 'Singles' Clubs
> 'Lonely Hearts' industry

**7** These are fleeting signs of community feeling e.g. disaster, street parties.

The answers:

> Care for elderly
> Work at home – 'electronic cottage'
> A job
> A dependent child
> Membership of a club

**8** Young people without a life structure take drugs to give them that structure.

Toffler calls it the '*Heroin Structure.*'

It centres on: Money
> A 'fix'
> Avoiding police

**9** He suggests schools should teach structure of everyday life:

> Allocation of time
> Personal uses of money
> Places to go for help
> How and where to complain

**10** In fact, says Toffler, there will be a new human being:

(a) Child will grow up in a non-child-centred society.
(b) Attention will be diverted to elderly.
(c) Adolescence will be shorter –
(all ages mixed in 'electronic cottage').
(d) Compulsory education shorter but more spread out.
(e) Workers less pre-programmed and faster on feet.
(Like difference between classical musician playing all written notes and a jazz improviser).

---

NOTES – THIRD WAVE

---

# REMEMBRANCE SUNDAY

1   Last Sunday/next Sunday was/is Remembrance Sunday.

2   Memories for many of: 1914–1918
                          1939–1945
                          Korea
                          Falklands
                          N. Ireland (and so on.)

3   (Teacher's personal memories e.g. National Service, father, brother, etc.).

4   1914–1918 – First World War.

    Millions died.

    Hopeless, mindless struggle. For what?

5   The play/film 'O What A Lovely War' really brings it home. Number of thousands killed in each battle and, often, the number of yards gained or even no gain at all.

6   1939–1945 – Second World War.

    Did it achieve anything?

    Did it win freedom for us?

7   But what was Britain to do?

    How does one deal with a Hitler?

    What would have happened if Nazism had won?

8   Some would say:

    'How much better are we now?'

    'Was the expense in lives justified?'

9   Many young people of your age say:

    'War is never justified,' and 'if there were another war I would refuse to fight.'

10  The strange thing is, when the call comes many young people are drawn by the adventure e.g. the Falklands. A number of young men (particularly) were itching to join in.

11  The fighting instinct is very strong in human beings – indeed in most animals.

    It was once needed for survival.

12  The human animal became 'top dog' because it developed weapons and traps.

**13** For the most part history is a history of wars.

It is wars that have changed history.

**14** Is war inevitable?

Either because we cannot help it,

or

because greed will always make people want what another country has.

**15** If, in the main, you think war evil, are there exceptions? Is war ever justified?

**16** And, of course, today there is added dimension – Nuclear Weapons.

**17** Each of you must think out his/her position.

**18** Would anyone like to lead the next Assembly with their views on this whole matter?

NOTES – REMEMBRANCE SUNDAY

# LIFE TOWARDS THE YEAR 2000

(Based on lecture by Professor Tom Stonier, Bradford University, in Ealing Town Hall, 1980).

**1** We are in middle of a new revolution.

Previously the Industrial – now the Electronic.

**2** Mechanisation made the feudal states non-viable.

Electronic age now makes nation states non-viable.

It is difficult to make a national product. Need for trans-national products.

**3** There has been a development of Super States:

Russia, U.S.A., China, that can survive on own.

Even that will pass.

**4** Stonier forecast democratisation of Russia.

Already happening in Poland. Signs also now in Russia.

**5** What are features of post-industrial society?
  - (i) Robots will replace the banal, mechanical.
  - (ii) Services sector will increase:
    - (a) Caring e.g. nurses.
    - (b) Individual attention – bars, hotels, shops.
  - (iii) Information available at press of button.
    (Teachers will no longer need to give information but advice, wisdom, re-levancy).

**6** When you know enough you can solve all problems.

**7** Much less emphasis on earning a living more on making a *life*.

**8** In 25 years' time only 10% of labour force will be needed to provide nation with needs.

**9** 10% will be in Leisure industry.

45%–50% in Knowledge industry.

**10** State will need to see every child has two things:
  - (a) Its own computer in home.
  - (b) A 'Grandmother.'

**11** Schools will need to teach five things:

How to: (a) Be an effective teenager.
  - (b) Be a good lover.
  - (c) Be a good parent.
  - (d) Grow old gracefully.
  - (e) Face death.

**12** (Discussion can then be invited on whole Assembly or paragraph 11 in particular).

---

NOTES – LIFE TOWARDS THE YEAR 2000

# MEMORY

**1**  Bob Hope's song:

'Thanks for the Memory.'

**2**  Marcel Proust, the French Novelist, wrote a book, translated as:

*'The Remembrance of Things Past.'*
(*A La Recherche Du Temps Perdu*).

**4**  Proust's memory is triggered by some simple act such as dipping a cake in his lemon tea.

This brings back his childhood when he used to dip his cake in the tea.

**5**  I wonder if this has ever happened to you?

You do something and it recalls for you an experience you had as a child.

You do not just recall that moment. It sparks off a picture of a whole period of your life.

**6**  A physical stimulus (such as Proust described) is a common experience for many people.

**7**  Memory is a wonderful thing.

(What are your favourite memories?)

**8**  It has two parts:

(1) To retain.
(2) To recall.

**9**  Experts tell us that we remember everything we have ever learnt. It is stored away in our own personal computer – the brain.

**10**  So there is little problem as far as retention is concerned.

**11**  The problem is to recall the information stored away.

**12**  How many times do you hear people say:

'It's on the tip of my tongue.'

'Hold on, I know the name begins with L.'

**13**  We are desperately trying to recall. We know the answer but we cannot bring it to the front of our minds.

**14**  So we have to use 'triggers.'

Proust used the physical but there are others e.g. mnemonics.

In music the four spaces in the treble clef are remembered as 'FACE.'

**15** Word association is similar:

EGBDF – For the lines in the treble clef = Every Good Boy Deserves Favour."

**16** Don't despise such devices. We need them, although we all have different blind spots.

Find your own way of remembering what is difficult for you,

e.g. the difference between:

Stationary and Station*e*ry – *e* stands for envelopes.

or

Receive: 'I' before 'E' except after 'C'.

**17** Sometimes we do not remember because it does not seem important.

What if I said 'come to me on the 3rd March 1995 at 3.00 p.m. and I will give you £5,000.'

Would you remember? I think you would.

**18** Memory can be trained.

No such thing as *a* bad memory.

But one can be bad at remembering this and good at remembering that.

**19** Memory can be important for exams.

Work at it, find your own system. If you always forget a particular fact or date or spelling, analyse it. Find an infallible way to remember:

e.g. What is the main religion of India? Is it Hindu or Muslim?

The next letter to I of India is 'H': answer Hindu.

**20** Fortunately God made our memories capable of blotting out the terrible and the nasty. We could not bear to have tragedies remain always vividly in our minds.

'Time heals – and forgets.'

**21** That is why our childhood memories are often of laughter, happiness and sunny days.

NOTES – MEMORY

# LEAVERS' ASSEMBLY

1    Listen to these words of St Paul to a young church at Philippi in Greece, or Macedonia as it was then called.

(Philippians, Chapter 4, verse 8)

'And now, my friends, all that is true, all that is noble, all that is just and pure, all that is lovable and gracious, whatever is excellent and admirable – fill all your thoughts with these things.'

2    I hope you have done well at school. That you regard your school life as a success.

3    Think back to coming here (age 11? 12?).

You were really just a child.

What a tremendous amount has happened?

You are now young men and women.

4    Not only have your bodies grown, your minds have developed too.

5    It has been very much our task – to open your minds, to help you make your own judgements, to think for yourself.

6    We are so often concerned with doing what is right, but it is what we are thinking that really matters.

7    Few crimes or evil deeds are unpremeditated. People plan them, ponder them, even savour them.

8    Our reading today used the expression: 'Fill your thoughts.'

What do you fill your thoughts with? Because our thinking makes us the people we are.

9    If your mind is full of evil, dishonesty, obscenity, treachery, hate, then you will be a despicable person.

10    St Paul advises: 'Fix your minds on the noble, the just, the pure, the lovable, the gracious – whatever is excellent and admirable.'

11    Never forget the word: excellent. It is sometimes despised nowadays. This school strives for Excellence.

12    You do the same. Never be content with the inferior, the second best.

Let it all be admirable and excellent.

13    Whatever you are going on to do: university, polytechnic, F.E., employment – stamp yourself with the motto:

'EXCELLENCE'

**14** Thank God for our minds and the power of thought. What pleasure, what satisfaction we can get from good, solid thinking.

**15** Never neglect your powers of thought and fill your mind with all that is excellent and admirable.

PRAYER

Examine us, O God, and know our mind. Purify our thoughts and guide us in ways of excellence.

As we approach the examinations give us clear minds, the power to study, the power to retain and the power to recall.

As our schooldays come to an end and we move into the wider world, help us to use our minds to the best advantage and so fulfil our potential both as individuals and citizens of the world.

NOTES – LEAVERS' ASSEMBLY

# LEAVERS' ASSEMBLY (Before 'A' Level exams)

**1** King Solomon was the son of King David who was the greatest King of Israel.

**2** Under David:
  (a) The country was united
  (b) All enemies conquered
  (c) Collected tribute money from all surrounding peoples and country became very rich.

**3** So Solomon was very lucky.

    (a) Good hardworking parent.
    (b) Set about doing great things himself e.g. building of Palace and Temple.

**4** Had reputation for great wisdom.

    (a) The Queen of Sheba travelled a distance to see him because of this reputation.
    (b) He sat at the gate of the city and pronounced judgements e.g. the two women with a Baby. One Baby had died and both claimed the one remaining was theirs.

        Solomon said: 'I will cut it in half.'

        One woman said 'Yes,' the real Mother said 'No, give it to her.'

**5** Solomon wrote a Book of Proverbs. I will quote from it:

(Proverbs, 6, 6–11)

Go to the ant thou sluggard: consider her ways and be wise, which having no guide, overseer or ruler, provideth her meat in the summer, and gathereth her food in the harvest. How long wilt thou sleep, O sluggard? When wilt thou arise out of thy sleep? Yet a little sleep, a little slumber, a little folding of the hands to sleep. So shall thy poverty come as one that travelleth and thy want as an armed man.

**6** To some people work is a dirty four-letter word.

**7** Study the ant – what a worker.

**8** Soon come the exams.

Are you very intelligent? Do you lack brains?

**9** There is no substitute for work (even at 'A' Level).

**10** This does not mean we should not know when to relax.

**11** Education is for the whole person.

That includes *Judgement*

        Knowledge of balance between work and leisure.

**12** In other words, like Solomon we need *wisdom*.

**13** Solomon told his son one basic thing:

        Respect for God is the beginning of wisdom.

**14** This is the basis of the best, the real, the wise life.

## OPTIONAL PRAYER

O God, look on us now as the stay in this school for many of us is drawing to a close.

As we look back we realise how different we are from the day we first entered this school.

Despite moments of sadness and conflict we are grateful for the many things we have enjoyed, for the friends we have made, and for the education we have received.

Go forward with us now into the world. Guide us in our careers. May what we have learned here stand us in good stead for the rest of our lives.

NOTES – LEAVERS' ASSEMBLY (Before 'A' level exams)

# INDEX